GROWING FRUIT

A PRACTICAL GUIDE TO GROWING TOP AND SOFT FRUIT

Chris Whitelock

GROWING FRUIT

A PRACTICAL GUIDE TO GROWING TOP AND SOFT FRUIT

THE CROWOOD PRESS

CONTENTS

INTRODUCTION

There are many reasons for gardeners to grow fruit in either their own gardens or their allotments. Being able to taste varieties that are not commonly available is one good reason. The apple variety 'Ashmead's Kernel' is considered by many to be the epitome of a dessert apple and yet it has long gone from most commercial orchards. Commercial fruit growers seek economy of scale, and often restrict their offering to a limited number of varieties for which flavour is a secondary consideration. Visual appeal, uniformity, and being able to store a variety for long periods without deterioration are more important than flavour or nutrition.

In addition, large-scale fruit producers, distributors and retailers all play their part in moving fruit long distances from faraway countries such as Chile and Australia to European markets. Even in the United Kingdom, fruit may be moved vast distances from the grower to the consumer via regional transport hubs operated by supermarkets and distributors. As we count the environmental cost of moving food around the globe in 'food miles', growing some of our own food locally makes sense. Whereas excessive transportation is a source of carbon dioxide, fruit trees and bushes absorb this gas and replace it with oxygen. If we grow our own food, we can also control the amount and type of pesticide, if any, that is used in its production.

Fruit trees and bushes are seldom purely productive – many also have ornamental attributes. For example, the cooking apple variety 'Arthur Turner' has received recognition on account of its striking pink blossoms in spring, but other apple varieties will also give a stunning display. Pears have beautiful white blossom, followed by glossy summer foliage that often colours richly in autumn. Cherries and plums add colour to the garden in spring, and fan-trained bush fruits such as redcurrants can make attractive garden features. Gooseberries can make a useful informal hedge, and a line of cordon fruit trees can be used as a garden division or screen. Fruit trees and bushes can be integrated into a garden as ornamental features without being banished to a 'fruit garden'. Combining edible and ornamental plants was one of the design principles of the cottage garden that has received renewed interest.

The presence of fruit trees and bushes can enhance the wildlife interest of a garden. This may or may not be welcome, as blackbirds are very efficient harvesters of soft fruit, but other birds can be extremely useful allies as they look out for caterpillars and aphids as a high-protein food source in spring. In autumn and winter, migrant fieldfares and redwings join our native birds in feeding off the remains of fruit on trees. Both fieldfares and redwings are on the RSPB 'red list' and need our help to ensure their survival. Being able to forage on fruit trees enables them to build up their fat reserves following their migration from Scandinavia. Small mammals such as hedgehogs and dormice will also relish fallen fruit as a vital source of winter sustenance.

The value of blossom as a source of sustenance for pollinators cannot be overestimated. Recent and justifiable concern for the decline in bee populations should encourage us to plant flowering trees and bushes. There are many species of bee that help with the pollination of tree fruits and bushes. The honeybee may be lauded for its industry, but many solitary bees play an important part in pollination and are less likely to be deterred by bad weather.

Lastly, fruit growing provides the gardener with an absorbing aspect of horticulture. It is not without its challenges: outbreaks of pest and disease and bad or unfavourable weather can be a source of frustration, but bumper crops of fruit harvested at the peak of perfection provide us with ample incentive to put the setbacks behind us and develop our skills. Involving the children or grandchildren in your endeavours will take advantage of their natural curiosity to educate them about how food grows, and will nurture healthy eating habits.

I have worked for over fifty years in horticulture and remain just as enthusiastic about the cultivation of fruit as when I started as an apprentice on a commercial production nursery. Over the time I have worked in the industry, new varieties, rootstocks and cultivation techniques have been developed. Some of these new developments are for the large-scale commercial grower, but many also favour the amateur gardener. Dwarfing rootstocks and trouble-free varieties make fruit cultivation a distinct possibility for gardeners who may be put off by a lack of space or expertise.

I have aimed this book at the amateur grower irrespective of their level of skill, knowledge and experience. I have tried to make it as up to date as possible, and have avoided making the subject unnecessarily complicated. Much of the content is based on my own experience of growing fruit in gardens and allotments using techniques that have given me good results.

Apple Arthur Turner is a decorative flowering tree as well as being productive.

CHAPTER 1

GETTING STARTED

Books on fruit growing written decades ago would offer all sorts of sage advice on how the gardener should position an orchard and fruit garden. The advice would be to pick a south-facing slope for maximum light and areas less likely to be troubled by spring frosts. The soil should be deep and well drained and not prone to waterlogging. If space is not an issue and you want to have large crops of fruit, that remains the best advice. If your garden is not large enough to accommodate a distinct orchard and soft-fruit garden, do not despair. As already mentioned, modern dwarfing rootstocks, compact varieties and systems of cultivation will enable you to have worthwhile crops of fruit in even a very small garden. Even without a garden, it is still possible to grow fruit on allotments or participate in a community orchard project.

No Garden Space

Allotments

Local authorities usually delegate the management of allotments to allotment societies. These societies set the rules and so it is advisable to check the rule book before planting fruit trees on your allotment. Some societies ban them outright (rare), but others may restrict the number of trees permitted on an individual plot. It is usual to permit only trees growing on dwarfing rootstocks to avoid problems associated with the shading of adjacent plots and the removal of trees following a change of tenancy. If the rules are unclear, check before spending money on trees that may have to be removed.

Community Orchards

The concept of community orchards was proposed by the Dorset-based charity, Common Ground, which encourages environmental improvement by community action. The charity has encouraged the establishment of hundreds of community orchards across the UK. A simple internet search will soon show the location of local ones. There is no definitive model of a community orchard: some are on land owned by local authorities and may be managed by a combination of local authority staff and volunteers, while other orchards may be privately owned but managed by a community group. The orchard may be an established one that has fallen into disrepair, or a new one planted from scratch.

Agreements must be made between the landowner and the community orchard group specifying responsibilities, liabilities, and the share of the produce.Many community orchards run into difficulties over conducting the necessary maintenance of the trees, and some orchard groups require members to commit to a certain number of hours per year to assist with orchard maintenance.

Orchard groups usually have a variety of social and promotional events such as wassailing and apple days. *The Community Orchards Handbook* by Clifford and King (two founders of Common Ground) provides some excellent advice on planning, establishing and managing a community orchard.

Columnar apple trees provide a convenient way of putting many trees in a comparatively small space.

In the Garden

Garden Orchards

If you have the space and want to be able to harvest a wide range of varieties of tree fruit, a small orchard can make a worthwhile and attractive garden feature. Although commercial orchards need to maximise cropping to remain profitable, the amateur grower can sacrifice a small proportion of the crop to achieve other functions. For example, grass is kept short to prevent it competing with the trees for water in nutrients. In the garden orchard, the grass can be kept longer and studded with wildflowers and bulbs to create a decorative display and benefit pollinators. Even small amounts of mistletoe can be tolerated in the garden orchard, valued not just for winter decoration but its berries are relished by many birds, particularly blackcaps and mistle thrushes (throstles).

A fan-trained gooseberry can make an attractive garden feature as well as being a convenient way of growing gooseberries.

Growing Fruit in Small Gardens

As building land becomes an increasingly scarce resource, modern gardens have become increasingly small. With space being a limitation, it is unlikely that it is possible to include a conventional orchard with wide tree spacings. However, a little careful thought and tree selection can enable a small garden to accommodate a selection of fruit trees and bushes without compromising its need to provide ornament and other functions. Walls and fences can be adorned with trained fruit trees, bushes, cane fruit and vines. Very dwarfing rootstocks such as M27 for apples and Quince 'Eline' for pears provide the owner of a small garden with the opportunity to grow fruit trees in restricted spaces.

Some apple varieties are available as 'columnar' or 'fastigiate' trees. These consist of a single main stem with very short branching, and can be planted very close together. Columnar trees such as the 'Ballerina' series have their own varieties; it is not possible to purchase a variety such as Laxton's Superb or Cox's Orange Pippin as a Ballerina tree. It is possible, however, to grow both varieties as oblique cordons.

Bush fruits such as redcurrants and gooseberries can be fan trained or grown as cordons against a wall, and will make attractive and remarkable garden features. As mentioned previously, gooseberries can make a useful informal garden hedge, the thorns providing useful security against intruders. Compact and dwarf varieties of bush fruit such as the blackcurrant

'Ben Sarek' and the blueberry 'Top Hat' are excellent choices if space is limited. Alpine strawberries, although their fruits are small, make an attractive groundcover and provide a delicious snack whilst weeding.

Growing Fruit in Containers

It is possible to grow trees, bush cane and vine fruit successfully in containers. For top fruits, trees grown on the M27 (apple), Quince 'Eline' (pear), VVA or Pixie (plum) and Gisela 5 (cherry) are ideal. The size of these will have a limiting effect on the ultimate size of the plant, which will need more careful management, including watering and feeding, than if grown directly in the soil. Choosing the right container is essential, and as a rule, the larger the better. Large containers will have greater stability and are less likely to dry out between waterings. A half-barrel or similar sized container is ideal for most fruits.

Choosing the right compost or growing medium is also important as it needs to support healthy growth over many years: choosing a low-grade growing medium is a false economy. Some high-quality composts will contain sterilised loam, which has the advantage of retaining water and plant nutrients better than soil-less growing media. The addition of loam to a growing medium will increase its bulk density and thereby increase the stability of the planted container.

A thin layer of crocking on the base of the container, such as broken terracotta, will ensure adequate drainage and protection against waterlogging in winter. Fruit trees on very dwarfing rootstocks will need permanent staking, and this still applies when grown in containers.

Plants grown in containers will need more regular watering than those grown in garden soil. Watering can be reduced by selecting a large container and incorporating sterilised loam into the growing medium. Planning to ensure containers are kept watered during summer holidays is essential; a drip irrigation system could be a wise investment if you take the time to calibrate it properly before you go away.

Frequent watering of a limited volume of growing medium will result in the loss of soluble plant nutrients (leaching), and these nutrients will need to be replenished using fertilisers. A granular slow-release feed can be added to the surface of the growing medium in spring, supplemented using liquid feeds during periods of strong active growth. A liquid feed made from comfrey provides a low-cost, organic and highly effective fertiliser.

Selecting Equipment

Fruit growing does not usually require a lot of expensive specialist equipment that does not have a use in general gardening. From experience, I recommend that you select high-quality equipment that gives good performance over a long period of time, rather than low-cost versions. The saying 'buy cheap, buy twice' usually rings true. It is also worth considering the after-sales support offered by the manufacturer, such as a long guarantee period and the availability of spares and servicing.

Secateurs

Secateurs are essential. There are two main types: bypass and anvil. Bypass secateurs cut using a scissor action and are best for making clean cuts in live wood. Anvil secateurs cut by means of a crushing action and will cope with thicker wood than bypass secateurs. The main disadvantage of anvil secateurs is that they do not make clean cuts, thus risking fungal infection. The main use for my anvil secateurs is for cutting up prunings destined for the bonfire or shredder. Some secateurs have a rotating handle that can reduce repetitive strain injury, and it is possible to buy models that are adapted for left-hand use. If money is no object, secateurs powered by a rechargeable battery or compressed air may be a suitable investment for the owner of a large orchard.

A quick word of advice about purchasing secateurs: avoid buying a pair with green handles. These may look attractive in the blister pack, but they may be hard to spot when put down in long grass. Red-, or red-and-white-handled tools are much easier to spot, and this can save a lot of frustration.

Never force secateurs to cut through thick stems. Manufacturers often overstate the cutting capacity of their goods. Forcing a pair of secateurs through a thick stem poses a great risk of twisting the cutting blade, rendering it useless. For cutting thicker stems, a good

Bypass secateurs make a clean pruning cut and are best for general pruning work.

pair of loppers is a worthwhile investment. Like secateurs, these will come with either a bypass or anvil cutting action, and will have a range of handle lengths. Long handles provide plenty of leverage for cutting but may be unwieldy in some situations. Beware of loppers with telescopic handles as these can often lack the necessary strength when fully extended.

Maintenance of Secateurs and Loppers

As much as it is important to buy good-quality secateurs and loppers, it is equally important to maintain them in good condition. The main tasks are cleaning, sharpening and lubrication. During use, secateurs and loppers accumulate plant saps that harden into a resinous layer that reduces the sharpness of the blades and may be a source of infection for plant pathogens, particularly viruses.

There is a variety of cleaning agents and materials that can remove the resin layer and maintain performance of the tools. Where there is a threat of disease transmission, such as silver leaf disease when pruning plums, the blades of pruning equipment should be cleaned with a sterilant when moving from one plant to another. It is usually enough to clean the blades at the end of each day. I favour the use of rubber blocks impregnated with abrasive powder. They are easy to use and remove any surface coating quickly and with minimal effort.

Moving parts should be lubricated with a light oil following use. I like to keep a small lubrication pen in a small metal tin, in which I also keep my sharpeners and a spare spring for my secateurs. A sharpener is an essential accessory for a decent pair of secateurs. Even with careful use, secateurs will blunt, which makes pruning unnecessarily hard work, and this may lead to repetitive strain injuries.

When sharpening secateurs and loppers it is important to remember that the blades are angled on one side only. The bevel angle is usually about 23 degrees (a quarter of a right-angle). Sharpeners that put an angle on both sides of the blade do more harm than good. I like to use diamond steel sharpeners, and those that use a sharpening block of a very hard material such as tungsten carbide. There are some excellent videos available on the internet, many by manufacturers demonstrating the correct technique for sharpening secateurs and loppers.

Pruning Saws

A good pruning saw is an essential piece of kit for managing fruit trees. A curve-bladed 'Grecian' saw is ideal for making cuts about shoulder height and is the best choice if you have space or budget for only one pruning saw in your tool kit. Fruit trees usually have hard wood and so saws with very large teeth may be hard to use as it may be difficult for the saw to bite into the wood. Japanese saws made from high-quality steel,

The curved blade of a Grecian pruning saw is particularly useful for pruning at shoulder height, and a scabbard is a safe addition for storage and carrying.

designed to cut on the back stroke, are both ergonomic and give an excellent finish.

If you need to cut branches that are higher than head height, a pole saw is essential as it does away with the potentially hazardous process of using a ladder whilst pruning. Pole saws usually come in lengths between 2 and 6m (6.5 and 20ft). Pole saws do not eliminate risk entirely, so a hard hat must be worn to prevent injury from falling branches, and goggles are advisable to prevent sawdust falling into your eyes. It is also important to keep pole saws well away from overhead power cables to avoid the serious risk of electrocution.

Maintenance of Pruning Saws

Some saws can be sharpened using a needle-point file, others that are induction-hardened cannot – however, these will retain their sharpness for a long period of time. A high-quality Japanese pruning saw is not cheap to buy and needs to be looked after so that it will repay its investment. Carefully cleaning the blade after use is important, and a thin layer of camellia seed oil applied to the dry blade will help to prevent rusting.

Ladders

Unless you are growing trees on a very dwarfing rootstock, it may be necessary to use a ladder for harvesting fruit. Domestic ladders are seldom fit for purpose, and the incorrect use and selection of ladders can lead to serious injuries. Tripod ladders are an excellent choice for outside use. They are remarkably stable, and the bases of their feet are designed to avoid sinking into soft soil. They are also light to carry and easy to position. I cannot recommend them too highly.

Sprayers

A sprayer may prove useful. Even if you are resolutely against the use of synthetic pesticides, the use of plant protection materials derived from natural materials such as plant oils may be acceptable. I have used these products with reasonable success and continue to do so. If you opt for a sprayer, avoid the very cheap ones as these seldom last; a good mid-range product with an extendable lance should do what you need of it admirably.

Buying Plants

Buying plants is a process that should not be done in haste. The internet has enabled specialist fruit-plant growers to connect with the public and offer a much wider selection of varieties than if they could only sell to a local market. There are several specialist fruit nurseries in the UK that offer a wide selection of varieties grafted on to a range of rootstocks, and which offer nationwide delivery. The information available on the websites of these nurseries allows for an informed choice. In addition there are several internet-based suppliers offering a wide range of plants including fruit plants. These general retailers offer a smaller selection than the specialist nurseries, but a combined order of fruit, ornamental plants and sundries could save on carriage costs. Some fruit nurseries offer a cash-and-carry facility, allowing customers to select and collect their fruit trees and bushes and obtain expert advice.

Garden centres often receive bad publicity, which may or may not be merited. The main advantage of using a local garden centre is that it may be possible to gain information on which varieties fare better in your locality. You may also be able to receive advice on looking after your plants, such as pruning and pest and

The retail sales area of a specialist production nursery usually offers a wide range of varieties, and expertise is often on hand.

An example of a poor bare-rooted plant with an inadequate root system. Surprisingly, with a lot of care, the tree survived and has borne fruit.

disease control. If you buy from a garden centre, select one that has knowledgeable staff. A good garden centre will offer a guarantee on hardy plants subject to reasonable conditions.

Supermarkets and discount stores may offer fruit trees and bushes as part of their seasonal gardening promotions. These can be a fraction of the cost of comparable plants offered by garden centres or nurseries, but they are usually offered in a very limited range of varieties, and essential information such as the rootstock is often missing. Also the care that the plants receive whilst they are in store is usually minimal.

Fruit trees and bushes can be purchased as bare-rooted specimens in winter, or as containerised specimens throughout the year. The advantage of bare-rooted specimens is that they are cheaper to buy, cost less to transport, and the root system can be examined prior to planting. The disadvantage of bare-rooted plants is that they can only be delivered and planted whilst dormant, and they need a little more care and attention than containerised plants. Bare-rooted plants need to be unpacked immediately on arrival and 'heeled in' in soil, or have the roots protected by a moist material such as sawdust or compost until they are ready for planting; on no account should the trees be placed in a warm environment, which will encourage premature growth.

Tree Forms

Fruit trees can be purchased in a variety of forms, or trained into these forms by formative pruning.

Bush Trees

The most common form for amateur growers is the bush tree, which consists of a single straight trunk, from which the main framework branches develop. Bush trees are usually grafted on to a dwarfing or semi-dwarfing rootstock. The advantage of having a short trunk is that the main fruit-bearing branches are closer to the ground, making pruning and harvesting much easier with the minimal use of ladders. The ultimate height and spread of a bush tree are influenced by the vigour of the rootstock, the pruning system used, the fertility of the soil, and the natural vigour of the variety. For example, trees of the popular cooking-apple variety 'Bramley's Seedling' will grow considerably larger than those of the compact variety 'Sunset' when grafted on the same rootstock and given identical pruning treatment on the same site.

A possible disadvantage of bush trees is that low branches can make mowing grass beneath the trees difficult.

Half-Standard Trees

Half-standard trees have a longer trunk than bush trees, making mowing beneath the canopy easier but pruning and harvesting more difficult. They are usually grafted on to vigorous or semi-vigorous rootstocks. Half-standard trees are popular for cider apples as these can be allowed to fall on to the ground before harvesting.

Standard Trees

The main stem of standard trees is clear of branches up to about 1.8m (6ft) in height. They are grafted on to a vigorous rootstock and were once a common sight in farm orchards where livestock could graze without being able to eat the foliage or fruit of the trees.

Fan-Trained Trees

Fan-trained trees have a short trunk from which the framework branches radiate in a two-dimensional pattern. They are primarily grown against walls, and have the advantage of not taking up too much space, and can be easily managed in terms of harvesting. They will need careful pruning, which is normally carried out in summer to restrict vigour.

Bush trees are convenient for picking and pruning as much of the tree can be reached from the ground.

Mowing under standard trees is easier than round a bush tree, but a ladder will be needed for pruning and harvesting.

Espalier trees are useful for training on a post-and-wire system; some pruning is necessary to restrict growth.

Even in winter, espalier trees can add structure to a garden.

Fan-trained trees are useful for growing against sunny walls for decorative effect as well as fruit production.

Espalier Trees

Espalier trees, like fan-trained trees, are grown as two-dimensional specimens that can be grown against a wall or trained on to a post-and-wire system. However, unlike fans whose branches radiate from a single point, the framework branches from an espalier are horizontal and grow out from the central trunk in pairs from different positions. Espalier trees are suitable for 'spur-fruiting' varieties that bear their fruit on small growths from the main branches. Like most restricted forms of fruit tree, the main pruning of espaliers is carried out in summer.

Cordon Trees

The most popular cordon trees are oblique cordons that are grown as single stems at an angle of 45 degrees from the ground. Growing the trees at this angle helps to restrict vegetative growth and promotes the formation of flower buds. Oblique cordons can be grown closely together, usually about one metre (3ft) apart. This enables a wide variety of varieties to be grown in a small area, and so they are ideal for small gardens. Cordons can be grown against a fence or on a post-and-wire system.

There are several variations of cordon trees that can be very decorative as well as productive. Double cordons have two framework branches instead of one and are trained into a V shape. Double cordons can be overlapped to form a decorative lattice effect, which makes a great screen. It is possible to grow cordons vertically, but it is worth considering that shoots are more vigorous and less productive when grown vertically rather than at 45 degrees. Vertical cordons may be trained to produce two or three framework branches. These are referred to as 'double' or 'triple' cordons. Spur-fruiting varieties of apple and pear make good subjects for cordon culture, though it is possible to grow plums by this method.

Stepover Trees

A stepover tree has one or two framework branches that are trained horizontally very close to the ground, so they can be stepped over with ease. They may form a decorative feature and a remarkable path edging. This system is best for apple and pear varieties that are moderately vigorous.

Cordon trees do not take up a lot of space and are an excellent way of growing many varieties where space is restricted.

Stepover trees make an attractive low hedge that is useful for making divisions in the garden.

Family Trees

A family tree is one where several (usually three) varieties of the same fruit have been grafted on to it. Family trees are usually bush trees and family trees of apples and of pears are quite common. The advantage of family trees is that several varieties are packed into the space occupied by one tree, and this offers both variety and improved pollination. The disadvantages of family trees include their purchase price, and the fact that the varieties may grow at different rates and have different systems of pruning. It is not difficult to graft new varieties of fruit on to a single-variety tree and get exactly the varieties that you want. Keep only one type of fruit per tree, graft apple varieties on to apple trees, and do the same with pears. Grafting techniques will be discussed in the section on tree propagation.

Maiden Trees

A maiden tree is one that has been grafted and grown for a season. It is usually a single unbranched shoot. A maiden tree can be trained into any one of the forms mentioned above. It has the advantage of being cheap to purchase, but will need careful formative pruning to get the desired tree form.

Planting Fruit Trees

There has been a lot of recent research into how to plant a tree correctly. The most important points are these:

- In most situations, a low stake is preferable to a tall stake as it permits the main stem of the tree to flex in the wind and this helps to reinforce the root system.
- Unless the soil is particularly poor, it is not necessary to apply a fertiliser to the planting hole (base dressing). Fertilisers can be applied to the soil surface (top dressing) when active growth commences.
- The application of liberal amounts of organic matter such as compost or farmyard manure to the planting hole is no longer deemed necessary. A case can be made for using organic matter in a poor sandy soil to improve water retention, but in most soils it is neither necessary nor desirable. A rich planting mixture used as a backfill in the planting hole creates a 'comfort zone' for the roots and discourages them from exploring the soil beyond the planting hole.
- A square planting hole discourages the spiralling of roots and so is often preferable to a round one.

The optimal time to plant fruit trees is during the dormant period when they are out of leaf. Autumn is a particularly good time as the soil is usually still warm from summer and adequate soil moisture favours root establishment. Bare-rooted trees are only available from late autumn onwards and must be planted before they come into growth.

Containerised trees (these are planted in the nursery and then lifted, potted, and grown on) can be planted throughout the year but benefit from autumn and winter planting as they are unlikely to suffer from water stress during the critical period of early establishment.

Planting should never be done in frozen or waterlogged conditions. A tree should never be planted in a location previously occupied by a tree of the same type. This is to prevent the tree suffering from 'specific replant disease', which may be caused by a variety of factors. The commonest cause of this disease is the build-up of pathogens in the soil. The effect of this disease on fruit trees is poor growth and possibly some

A low stake can be used to enable the stem to flex in the wind. This will help to strengthen the root system.

rotting of the root system. The use of mycorrhizal fungi when planting could have some effect on mitigating the disease. The best prevention is not to plant a tree on the site of a previous one.

For containerised trees, the planting hole should be three times the width of the container the tree was growing in, and should be deep enough to ensure that the top of the rootball is at soil level. For bare-root trees, the 'soil mark' on the main stem must be level with the soil. In heavy or compacted soils, the base of the planting hole should be loosened to the depth of a digging fork to assist root penetration. Whilst the hole is being dug, the roots should be soaked prior to planting. Immersing the roots for about fifteen minutes should suffice. If spiralled roots are evident when the pot of a containerised tree is removed, the roots should be gently teased out. Badly spiralled roots should be cut with a sharp knife to prevent spiralling continuing. The roots of bare-rooted trees should be spread out as evenly as possible.

When the tree is placed in the planting hole, a piece of wood with a straight edge can be used to check that the planting depth is correct. If the planting hole is too shallow this can lead to the plant drying out during establishment, and this could prove fatal. If the planting hole is too deep this can result in root rot. If the scion is in contact with the soil, it may start to produce roots and effectively bypass the rootstock. This will render the rootstock useless in its key function of mitigating growth, resulting in excessive vigour at the expense of fruit development and tree management.

The excavated soil is used to backfill the planting hole. This is gently consolidated to prevent the development of air pockets that could become filled with cold air that could damage the roots. Gently shaking the main stem of a bare-root tree during planting helps to consolidate the soil. Planting bare-rooted trees is often easier with two people.

Once the tree is in the soil, a light mulch will help to protect the roots from frost and conserve moisture. Chipped bark is an ideal mulch material, but coir 'mulch mats' or a cardboard collar made from strong cardboard will work equally well. Fleece also makes a great mulch material and depending on where you live, can be obtained for minimal cost as it is often a waste

During planting, a planting board can be used to ensure that the tree is planted at the correct depth.

The graft union is where the scion and the root stalk join. It is usually seen as a swelling at the base of the tree.

product. Material such as bark should be applied as a 5cm (2in) thick layer, and it should not be allowed to come in contact with the main trunk of the tree.

A low stake hammered into the ground at 45 degrees allows the main stem to flex in the wind and avoids damaging the root system. Many trees on dwarfing rootstocks need permanent staking; ones on more vigorous rootstocks may need staking for two or three years. The tree needs to be fastened to the stake using a tree tie – using string or cord can cause serious damage to the delicate bark and can severely restrict growth or possibly even kill the tree. Because the main stem of the tree becomes thicker as it grows, the tree tie will need to be checked regularly and slackened as necessary to prevent 'girdling' of the tree.

Protection of Newly Planted Trees

In rural areas where wild rabbits feed, the use of a rabbit or hare guard is essential. These spiralled pieces of plastic protect the tender young bark and prevent rabbits from gnawing it. In winter when food is scarce, the thin bark of trees is particularly nutritious to rabbits. A single rabbit can kill several trees in a single day and so the guards must be placed immediately after planting. Leaving the trees unprotected even for a single night could prove a costly mistake.

Deer can be very destructive. Deer damage includes eating foliage, fruit, the young stems of trees, and the bark in winter. Male deer may rub the bark of trees with their heads to remove the velvet on new antlers. This is known as 'fraying'. The antlers can make vertical cuts in the bark and peel it off, causing considerable damage.

Deer guards vary greatly in their design and cost. They may be as simple as rolls of metal mesh, or elaborate designs made in a forge. If large numbers are required, a simple structure can be made from timber, barbed wire and sheep fencing. If grazing animals, including sheep, are allowed in the orchard, deer guards are essential. Sheep are particularly adept at damaging bark.

Watering

Irrigation is an essential consideration to ensure the survival of newly planted trees. The application of a mulch at planting time will help to minimise water loss from the soil as well as suppressing the growth of weeds that can rob moisture. The amount of water required by a newly planted tree will depend on its size, rate of growth and the texture of the soil. The free-draining nature of sandy soils means that more frequent watering is necessary than on clay or silty soils. Trees are best watered thoroughly and infrequently rather than with a daily dribble. Frequent light watering encourages surface rooting, but allowing the soil to dry out between thorough waterings encourages deep rooting as the roots follow the moisture in the soil.

A purpose-built deer guard protects young trees from deer damage.

CHAPTER 2

PROPAGATING FRUIT TREES

Most fruit trees are propagated by grafting a piece of wood or bud of the desired variety on to a compatible rootstock. Growing a fruit tree from seed is a pure gamble that you are likely to lose, as there is no guarantee that the resultant seedling will have any of the desirable characteristics of the parent tree. Most seedlings will have two parents: the female parent that bore the seed, and the male that supplied the pollen. Occasionally raising a seedling tree will pay dividends. Some of the most popular fruit varieties came about because a discarded core grew into a tree with excellent fruit. The apple variety Cox's Orange Pippin was discovered as a chance seedling at Colnbrook near Slough. It had probably come from the seed of the variety 'Margil'. The name 'pippin' in an apple variety denotes its origin as a chance seedling.

It is possible to raise apple trees from cuttings and thereby replicate the genetic characteristics of the parent plant, but this is not a practical proposition. Apple-tree cuttings are difficult to root, and without the constraint of a dwarfing rootstock will make very large trees that are too big for garden or orchard use. Grafting requires skill, but this can be acquired through diligence and practice.

Grafting

There are several good reasons for learning to graft. The first is that it can save a lot of money, as rootstocks are much cheaper to purchase than grafted trees. The second is that it is possible to graft a particular variety not easily obtainable from usual sources; this may be the case with an unnamed variety of fruit tree that you wish to replicate. The third reason is that it provides you with the ability to add an additional variety of fruit into one of your existing trees. For example, it would be possible to graft a branch of a cooking apple into a dessert variety, and both varieties could pollinate each other. It is also possible to change an apple variety into another by making multiple grafts into the framework shoots. The last and by no means least reason is that it is rewarding to graft your own trees and get a sense of pride when you make your first successful graft.

However, a word of caution is needed: grafting requires a sharp knife, and a lot of practice is needed to become proficient. Keep a first-aid kit handy when you are practising!

It is possible to buy specialist grafting knives. These should be made from a high-carbon steel that can keep its edge well after sharpening. The bevel should be on one side only. A good grafting knife must be kept clean and sharp to make precise cuts that heal quickly and avoid the transmission of disease. A good sharpening kit suitable for knives with a single bevel is an essential accessory for grafting knives. An alternative to a grafting knife is a craft knife with sharp, replaceable blades.

Whichever grafting method is used, you will need tape to bind the scion to the rootstock. Traditional gardeners may use raffia, but my personal preference is Parafilm tape that is stretchable and forms a tight, waterproof binding that can biodegrade. Parafilm grafting tape is reasonably cheap and can be easily sourced, usually via the internet. Some experts will suggest the use of cut-up freezer bags, PVC, or even cellophane tape. These materials may work, but there is little sense in using inferior products when Parafilm is relatively cheap, immeasurably more effective, and easier to use.

Rootstocks for grafting can be obtained from a specialist fruit nursery. These are usually sold in bundles as bare-rooted plants and so are only despatched in winter. On receipt, the rootstocks should be 'heeled in' or potted so that the roots are protected from frost and desiccation. The different rootstocks and their uses will be discussed in the sections for each type of fruit.

There are many different techniques of grafting with their own relative advantages; however for the sake of brevity, this chapter will cover just the most popular techniques. Grafting can be learned in a variety of ways. In rural areas, orchard groups will organise their own grafting workshops; alternatively some nurseries and horticultural colleges will offer short courses on grafting. If attending a course (highly recommended) is not possible, there are some excellent instructional videos available on the internet. The People's Trust for Endangered Species offers some excellent videos on orchard skills, including grafting. There are many others by experienced nursery propagators and fruit growers. It is worth seeing several to get as much information as possible.

When grafting in winter, it is usual for the wood of the cultivated variety (scion wood) to be collected whilst fully dormant in late winter. Cuttings are taken from one-year-old growth ideally about pencil thickness. One-year-old wood is normally unbranched and will not usually have fruit buds. Once the scion wood has been harvested, it is cold stored in either a fridge (not freezer) or in a cool outside location such as the north side of a building. Strong growing shoots are the best choice for scions as these ensure grafting success.

It is important to prevent scion wood from drying out whilst in cold storage. Wrapping bundles of the scion wood in very slightly moistened paper tissue and putting them in Ziploc bags can help to keep them moist. Treating the cut ends with a wound sealant can further reduce moisture loss from the wood. However, it is important to avoid over-wetting the paper to prevent the wood rotting in storage.

The reason for the cold storage of scion wood is to delay the opening of the buds and to keep them dormant for grafting. The rootstock, on the other hand, should be breaking dormancy and starting growth. A dormant scion can draw sap from an active rootstock and come into growth. The best time to winter graft is when growth begins on the rootstocks: this may be a slight swelling of the growth buds and/or new root growth. The method of grafting will depend on the relative thickness of the scion wood and rootstock, and the experience and preference of the propagator.

Whichever grafting method is used, it is essential for the thin layer of cambium cells in the rootstock and scion to be in close contact and to fuse. The cambium layer can be seen as a very thin layer of green wood situated just beneath the bark.

Whip-and-Tongue Grafting

Whip-and-tongue grafting is the winter graft most favoured by professional propagators. In this graft, two matching oblique cuts are made into both the scion and rootstock. Ideally the scion and rootstock should be the same diameter to maximise cambial contact. It is important to make clean cuts using a sharp knife; 'whittling' will result in uneven concave cuts with less opportunity for success. A simple whip graft is made by putting these two cuts together (ensuring that the scion is pointing in the correct direction) and binding them securely. The success of the graft is greatly increased by cutting two 'tongues' into the rootstock and scion. If the scion is thinner than the rootstock, the two should be aligned on one side only, as centring the scion will result in no cambial contact and the graft failing.

Once the rootstock and scion have been joined, the graft can be made more secure and waterproof using grafting tape. Do not worry about overlapping the tape: this can be done several times. Parafilm tape should be stretched slightly and will adhere to itself. Polythene film is less elastic and needs to be secured

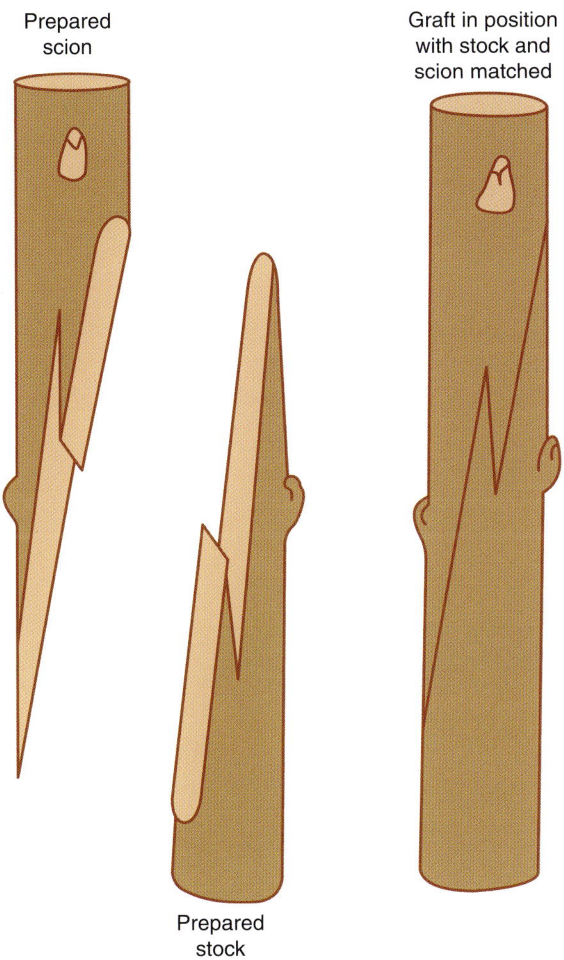

Whip-and-tongue graft.

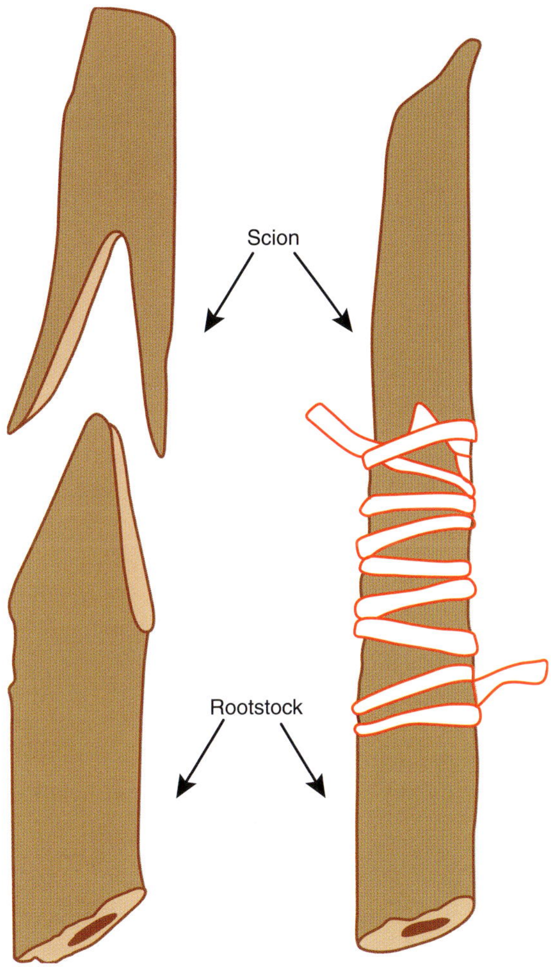

After the rootstock and scion have been joined, the saddle graft can be sealed using grafting tape or a rubber band.

by knotting. Some propagators will strengthen the graft union using rubber bands to further bind the rootstock and scion. My preference is to use a layer of grafting wax or pruning compound as a layer over the grafting tape. The scion should be shortened to three or four buds above the graft union, and a layer of pruning compound over the cut end of the scion will help to minimise water loss.

Saddle or V Grafting

Saddle or V grafting is a favoured method with some propagators but is less common than the whip-and-tongue graft. An inverted V cut is made in the rootstock, and a V is cut in the scion. With practice, it is possible to make matching cuts and get good cambial contact. Like whip-and-tongue grafts, if the scion is thinner than the rootstock, the scion and rootstock should be flush on just one side. With both types of graft, it is possible to have a scion thinner than the rootstock but not the other way round.

It is possible to make effective saddle or V grafts using a grafting tool. These tools are easily obtainable from internet suppliers, and provided that the blades are kept clean and sharp, reasonably accurate cuts can be made. I have obtained a very acceptable rate of success using the grafting tool photographed. The advantage of using a grafting tool is that hands and

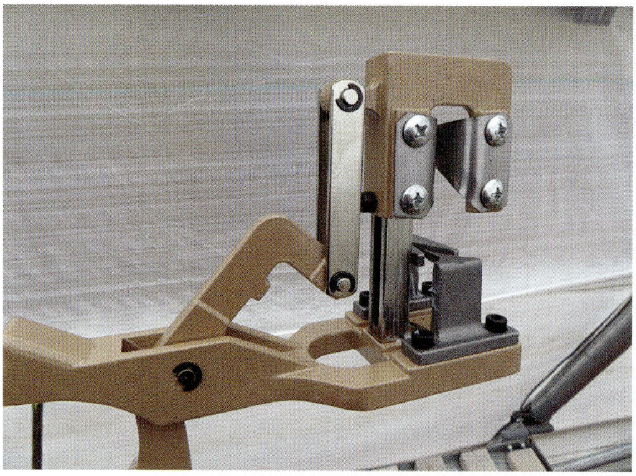

Grafting normally requires a lot of skill and the use of a very sharp knife. This grafting tool makes the task easier and safer.

blades are kept a safe distance apart, thus minimising accidents. After the scion and rootstock have been joined, the graft union is treated the same as for whip-and-tongue grafts.

For both whip-and-tongue and saddle grafts, if possible, the grafted plants should be moved to a protected location – an unheated glasshouse or polythene tunnel is ideal.

Cleft Grafting

There are two important advantages of cleft grafting: the first is that it allows comparatively thinner scions to be grafted on to thicker rootstocks, and the second is its pure simplicity. It is particularly useful for regrafting established trees, including the addition of a new variety into the branch framework. In this simple method, a single vertical cut is made across the diameter of the rootstock. The scion is cut to a thin wedge that is inserted into a vertical cut in the rootstock. The thicker part of the wedge is placed on the outside, and as the bark is thinner on the scion, it is inserted with a very slight recess into the rootstock to ensure the cambium layers align.

After insertion, the graft should be protected using wax or a wound sealant, and grafting tape applied to prevent the entry of water and pathogens.

If the graft is not successful, all is not lost. When the rootstock has put on new growth, it can be bud grafted, as described in the next section.

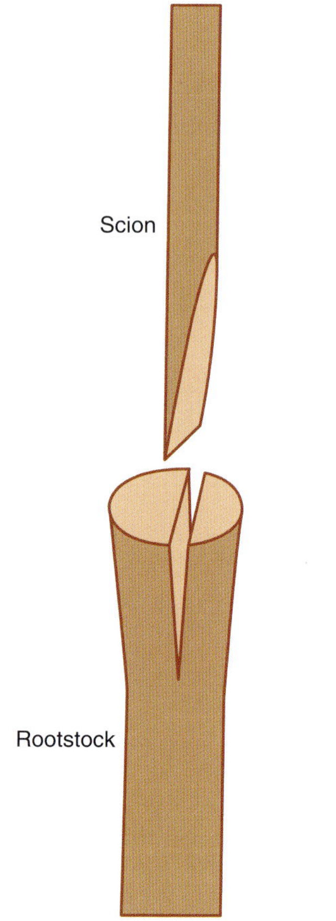

In a cleft graft it is advisable to align the cambium of the rootstock and scion on one side only.

Bud Grafting

Bud grafting, or 'budding', is the most widely used method of propagating fruit trees. It is quicker and easier than the winter grafting techniques described in previous sections. The scion wood does not need to be cold stored; a lot of trees can be grafted from a limited amount of scion material and the operation can be carried out 'in the field'. Bud grafting is carried out in late summer when the axillary buds of the scion variety have started to ripen following the cessation of extension growth. This is usually late July to mid-August in the UK. The rootstocks must be kept well watered to promote sap flow.

Budding involves excising a single bud and inserting it into a rootstock. As with winter grafting, a stem of

Bud grafting is usually carried out in the field during the summer months. A single bud of the cultivated variety is inserted into a suitable rootstock.

Tying in a bud graft. Nurseries use a specialist budding tape, but cut-up freezer bags are a reasonable substitute.

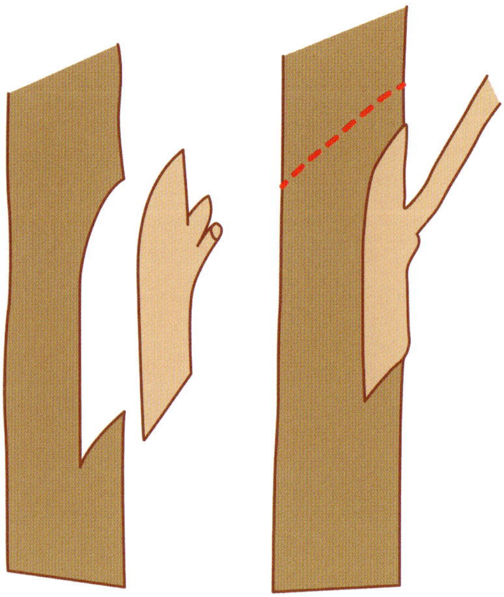

An excised bud from the scion wood is inserted into a corresponding cut in the rootstock and then bound. When the bud has taken, the rootstock is cut just above the inserted bud

Transverse view of a bud graft. The leaf petiole (stalk) is removed after the bud has been tied in. When dormant, the rootstock is cut just above the inserted bud along the dotted line.

current season's growth is selected. This is best done early in the morning when moisture levels are highest. The foliage is removed quickly so that moisture loss is minimised. The petioles are retained as these provide handles to hold the bud whilst grafting.

There are two variations of budding: chip budding and T budding. Chip budding involves the removal of a small cavity in the rootstock into which the scion bud is inserted. This is the most common form of budding for fruit trees.

T budding involves making a T cut in the rootstock, peeling back the bark, and inserting an excised bud. In both budding techniques the rootstock is left unpruned, allowing its foliage to draw up sap into the inserted bud, and the bud is tied in with tape immediately after insertion.

The fusion of the cambium layers of the scion and rootstock will take place over the next few weeks. It may be possible to remove the grafting tape in autumn, but the natural elasticity of Parafilm enables it to stay in place until spring without causing any harm.

If the inserted bud starts to swell and show signs of activity in the spring, the rootstock can be cut back just above this bud to make it the dominant bud and encourage strong scion growth.

All forms of grafting require skill, but this can be developed through practice. Winter grafting can be practised easily on prunings, and a few cut stems of willow can provide plenty of material to practise chip or T budding.

Plant Breeders' Rights

Some varieties of plant, including fruit trees and bushes, are protected by plant breeders' rights. These rights are like a copyright and protect the variety breeder or licence holder by prohibiting the propagation of a protected variety. This prohibition covers propagation for your own use or resale. Protected varieties will usually have a label stating if plant breeders' rights are applicable. Plant breeders' rights provide the breeder with a financial reward for the work involved in breeding and introducing the new variety, and are essential if we are to benefit from new varieties.

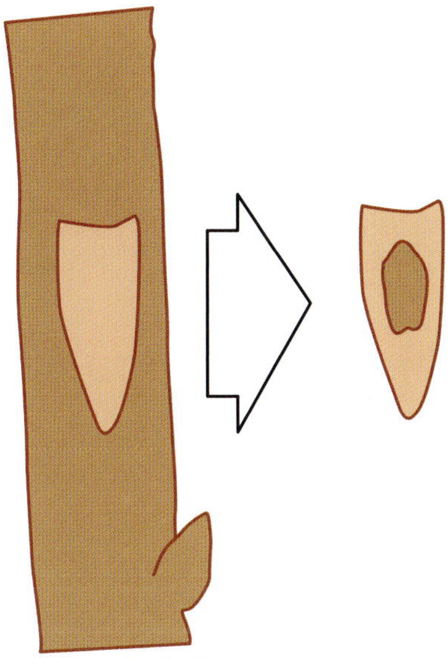

T budding step 1: A 'shield shape' piece of wood containing a bud is removed.

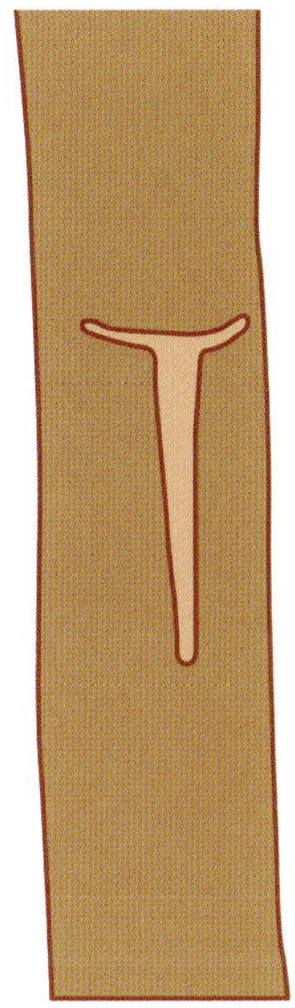

T budding step 2: An inverted 'T' is cut into the wood.

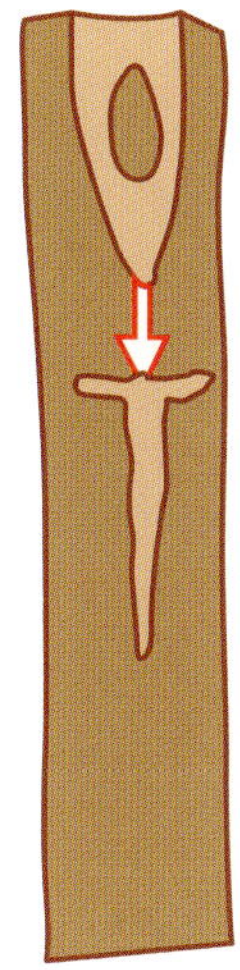

T budding step 3: The 'shield' is inserted into the T cut.

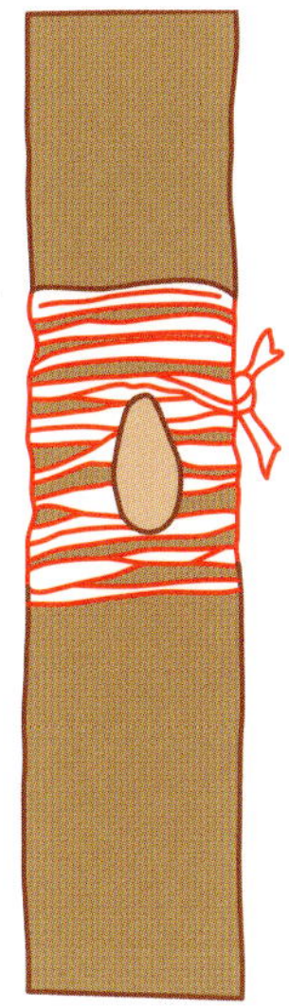

T budding step 4: The bud is tied into place.

CHAPTER 3

GROWING APPLES

It is believed that there are about 7,000 varieties of apple in worldwide cultivation, of which about 2,500 have been raised in the UK. The orchard apple *Malus domestica* originated in Kazakhstan, from hybrids and selections of the wild apple species *Malus sierversii*. The taxonomy of *Malus domestica* is very complicated and still not fully understood by botanists. Hybrids between *Malus sierversii* and four other local species of Malus developed. This hybridisation accounts for the genetic complexity of cultivated apples. Seeds of these early apples were transported in saddle bags and the digestive systems of horses along the Silk Roads to Europe. As early as 1000BCE reference was made about grafting productive varieties of fruit by Chinese and European horticulturists. The Greeks loved apples and so did the Romans, who may have introduced apples to Britain. The Romans certainly had named varieties of apple that they propagated by grafting. The heritage variety 'Dacio' can be traced back to the Romans. Following their conquest of England, the Normans established orchards for eating and cider apples. In 1204, mention is made of the apple variety 'The Pearmain' growing in Norfolk.

Henry VIII established apple orchards in Kent and sent his chief fruiterer, Richard Harris, over to France to learn more about fruit growing. Harris returned with scions of new varieties to plant in the new orchards. The introduction of new varieties continued largely through the discovery of chance seedlings, but the Victorian enthusiasm for science and innovation led to many more varieties being developed as a result of planned breeding programmes. Head gardeners would compete to produce new varieties of apple to impress their employers. Organisations such as the Royal Horticultural Society promoted this enthusiasm through their programme of shows, and their recognition of varieties that showed merit. Many of our popular apple varieties can be traced back to the Victorian era.

Apples were exported to former colonies such as the United States, Canada, Australia and New Zealand, and the development of new varieties that suited local conditions continued. Apple varieties from the USA include 'Golden Delicious', 'Jonagold' and 'Honeycrisp'. 'Granny Smith' and 'Cripps Pink' (Pink Lady) came from Australia, and 'Gala' from New Zealand. Mainland European countries also contributed to the development of new apple varieties. Horticultural research establishments all over the world, such as the East Malling Research Station in Kent, embarked on systematic breeding programmes to produce apples suitable for the commercial grower.

The introduction of new varieties is a never-ending process, and each year nursery catalogues boast of new introductions developed by breeding programmes or chance seedlings. As well as developing new varieties, there are considerable efforts being made to catalogue and preserve 'heritage' varieties. These heritage varieties may have arisen from chance seedlings and grown without formal recognition in local orchards. Often lacking in cosmetic beauty, these heritage varieties have other redeeming qualities such as disease resistance and the ability to thrive in difficult environments.

Preserving heritage varieties is not merely horticultural nostalgia: their genes could make a useful resource for the breeding of new varieties. The unsung heroes of the campaign to preserve heritage varieties are local orchard groups and charities such as the Orchard Project. These organisations often run promotional events through the year and are worth attending for anybody with an interest in apple growing. Representatives of these organisations provide a wealth of information on apple growing based on their considerable practical experience.

Choosing Varieties

Specialist fruit nurseries can offer a wide variety of choice when it comes to varieties as they can offer their stock on a nationwide basis. Garden centres have to be more restricted to 'best sellers', which may not necessarily be the best varieties to suit your needs. Customers may seek varieties with which they are familiar, such as Cox's Orange Pippin and Granny Smith. Cox's Orange Pippin is notoriously difficult to grow on account of its susceptibility to disease, and Granny Smith needs a sunny Australian climate to ripen properly. The same problem with climate arises with the supermarket favourite Cripps Pink, which is given the marketing name 'Pink Lady'. Cripps Pink is not grown in the UK on account of the climate. Fortunately, amongst the hundreds of apple varieties offered for sale, it is possible to pick ones that are ideally suited to individual needs. Selecting varieties from those offered in supermarkets can create problems. The United Kingdom grows only 30 per cent of its apples, with many coming from countries with a different climate.

Apple sales at an RHS garden provide a great opportunity to try out varieties not normally offered by the supermarkets.

Fortunately, there are still many fruit farms that grow a range of varieties and will offer customers the opportunity to sample the fruit before buying. A local fruit farm will grow varieties that fare well in its locality and will give a much better pointer for suitable varieties than a supermarket. Some of the gardens of the Royal Horticultural Society (RHS) have orchards with a wide selection of varieties. The fruit from these orchards is often sold when in season to raise revenue. Some of the varieties will be obscure and not commonly available, but many can be purchased from specialist nurseries. Local orchard groups may hold promotional events including 'apple days', in which many varieties are displayed and possibly sampled.

The catalogues of several of the larger specialist nurseries have detailed descriptions of the varieties that they offer. This can be useful, but a word of caution is necessary, as words such as 'delicious' can be subjective. I have read descriptions full of gushing praise for varieties I find unappealing, while ones that I favour will not be to everyone's liking.

It is possible to list some of the main criteria for selecting apple varieties.

Use

Some apple varieties are predominantly suitable for cooking and are often called 'culinary' varieties. The popular variety 'Bramley's Seedling' is the foremost culinary variety. They are assessed according to their acidity and characteristics when cooked. Some hold their shape when cooked and are good for baking, while others will turn into a purée when cooked and make a useful pie filling or sauce. Some varieties are described as dual-purpose and are suitable for cooking and eating fresh. The deservedly popular apple varieties 'Charles Ross' and 'James Grieve' fall into this category. Apples of these varieties are usually picked slightly underripe for cooking, or are allowed to ripen fully for maximum sweetness. Apples usually sweeten after a period of storage, and even Bramley's Seedling can be eaten uncooked around Easter.

Dessert apples can be eaten uncooked and unsweetened. The flavours range from 'aromatic' varieties such as Ashmead's Kernel with its complex range of flavours including pear drop, to the sweeter, juicier types that are gaining popularity. Apples such as Honeycrisp and Gala fall into this category. Dessert-apple varieties outnumber culinary ones by a large margin.

Pollination

Most apples are unable to set fruit on their own pollen and are called 'self-sterile'. This is common in the plant world and is a mechanism to prevent inbreeding and encourage genetic diversity in the species. Most apple varieties are considered self-sterile, but some are reliably self-fertile and can set fruit without a pollination partner. The modern dessert apple varieties 'Scrumptious' and 'Cox's Orange Pippin Self-Fertile' are two good examples of self-fertile varieties. To confuse the issue, some apple varieties are considered 'partially self-fertile'. Partially self-fertile apple varieties can set a limited amount of fruit on their own pollen, but cropping is enhanced by the introduction of a pollination partner. You will find conflicting information about partially self-fertile varieties from different catalogues, so these varieties are best treated as self-sterile to be on the safe side.

Apple Scrumptious is an excellent modern variety that is truly delicious and is self-fertile.

Triploid Apple Varieties

Ashmead's Kernel
Belle de Boskoop
Blenheim Orange
Bramley's Seedling
Gravenstein
Jonagold
Jupiter
Orleans Reinette
Ribston Pippin
Suntan
Warner's King
Washington

Apple Jonagold is a very heavy cropping variety but is unsuitable as a pollinator because it is triploid.

An additional complication concerning the pollination of apples is the existence of triploid varieties. Most apple varieties have seventeen pairs of chromosomes, but in triploid varieties the chromosomes are in threes rather than pairs. Being triploid usually gives the plant more vigour than its diploid counterparts and this often results in improved disease resistance, the ability to tolerate poor growing conditions and larger fruit size. These are important advantages for the grower. The possible downsides are that triploid varieties have sterile pollen, and their vigour may result in trees that are too large for a restricted space.

Recent research by East Malling Research Station in Kent has discovered that over 10 per cent of UK apple varieties are triploid. The surprise was the heritage variety 'Ashmead's Kernel', which was known to be a poor pollination partner.

There is a common myth that triploid apples require two pollinators – however, they require only one, but as their pollen is effectively sterile, triploids cannot pollinate their pollinators. If the pollinating variety is self-sterile, a third variety will be needed for pollination. For example, a Bramley's Seedling apple can be pollinated by the self-fertile variety Scrumptious. Both trees will be able to crop. However, if a variety such as Discovery, which is not fully self-fertile, were selected to pollinate the Bramley, the Bramley would be pollinated by Discovery but not the other way round. An additional variety such as Spartan would enable all three trees to be pollinated.

To achieve successful pollination, varieties in a pollination partnership must flower at approximately the same time. Apples can be classified as early, mid-season and late flowering. Early-flowering varieties are not necessarily early cropping. For example, the popular early apple 'Worcester Pearmain' is a mid-season-flowering variety yet is an early cropper.

The Royal Horticultural Society (RHS) places apple varieties into seven flowering groups ranging from one (earliest) to seven (latest). Pollination partner varieties must be in the same or an adjacent group to be effective. For example, a variety in pollination group three can be pollinated by one in groups two, three or four. An apple in pollination group two will not be pollinated effectively by a variety in pollination groups four to seven. Fortunately, most apple varieties fall within pollination groups two to four. There is only one variety listed in group seven (Crawley Beauty), which can be pollinated by others in group six.

Like many other plants, apple flowers use biochemical inhibitors to reject their own pollen. In some cases where their genetic information is very similar, certain varieties will not pollinate each other. Fortunately, incompatibility in apples is rare and restricted to a few instances. Cox's Orange Pippin shares its genes with many varieties and will not form a pollination partnership with Kidd's Orange Red, Holstein or Suntan for that very reason. Similarly, Crispin (Mutsu) and Golden Delicious are not suitable pollination partners.

Crab apples grown either for fruit or garden ornament make excellent pollinators for apples, and there are plenty of varieties to choose from. Worthy of

Crab apples can be ornamental and productive and make excellent pollinators for apple varieties.

mention are Golden Hornet, John Downie, Floribunda and Evereste.

Pollinating Insects

There has been a lot of justifiable concern about the loss of pollinating insects, caused by a variety of reasons including pesticide use, climate change and habitat destruction. This has stimulated a lot of useful research into the value and preservation of these vital species. Research by the University of Reading carried out in Kent orchards concluded that over 25 species of bee and hoverfly were active on apple blossom. Honeybees were frequent visitors to the orchards, even if hives were not placed in them. The most common pollinating insects in the Kent orchards were Andrenid bees, which include several solitary ground-dwelling species.

The small, black St Mark's fly, also known as the Hawthorn fly, is another important pollinator for tree fruit. Adults emerge around the time of the feast of St Marks and can be seen in large numbers. Larvae of this fly are ground-dwellers, feeding on rotting organic matter and plant roots.

Commercial growers often site beehives or bee nesting boxes in their orchards to improve pollination. This may involve an agreement in which the orchard owner is paid in honey. Many bee conservation groups offer excellent advice on how to select, position and maintain bee nesting boxes. Buying from these charities helps to promote a worthy cause and ensures that the nesting box is fit for purpose. Nesting boxes manufactured abroad may not be suitable for UK bees. Maintenance of the nesting box is essential to prevent parasitism of the bee larvae.

Apple Pollination Groups Based on RHS Data

Varieties marked AGM have been awarded an Award of Garden Merit by the Royal Horticultural Society.

Group One (earliest flowering)

'Gravenstein' (triploid)
'Lord Suffield'
'Stark Earliest' (syn. 'Scarlet Pimpernel')
'Vista Bella'

Group Two

'Adam's Pearmain'
'Alkmene' AGM (syn. 'Early Windsor')
'Baker's Delicious'
'Beauty of Bath'
'Beauty of Blackmoor'
'Bismarck'
'Bolero' (syn. 'Tuscan')
'Brownlees Russet'
'Cheddar Cross'
'Christmas Pearmain'
'Devonshire Quarrenden'
'Downton Pippin'
'Egremont Russet' AGM
'George Cave'
'Golden Spire'
'Idared' AGM
'Irish Peach'
'Keswick Codling'
'Laxton's Early Crimson'
'Lord Lambourne' AGM
'Maidstone Favourite'
'McIntosh'
'Red Melba'
'Merton Charm'
'Michaelmas Red'
'Norfolk Beauty'
'Owen Thomas'
'Reverend W. Wilks'
'Ribston Pippin' AGM (triploid)
'Rosette'
'Ross Nonpareil'
'Saint Edmund's Pippin' AGM
'Striped Beefing'
'Trinity'
'Warner's King' AGM (triploid)
'Washington' (triploid)

Group Three

'Acme'
'Alexander' (syn. 'Emperor Alexander')
'Allington Pippin'
'Arthur Turner' AGM
'Barnack Orange'
'Belle de Boskoop' AGM (triploid)
'Bladon Pippin'
'Blenheim Orange' AGM (triploid)
'Bloody Ploughman'
'Bountiful'
'Bowden's Seedling'
'Bramley's Seedling' AGM (triploid)
'Bright Future'
'Brownlees Russett'
'Captain Kidd'
'Captain Tom'
'Catshead' (triploid)
'Charles Ross' AGM
'Cobra'
'Core Blimey'
'Court of Wick'
'Cox's Orange Pippin'
'Crispin' (syn. 'Mutsu') (triploid)
'Cowngold' (triploid)
'Discovery' AGM
'Eden'
'Elstar' AGM
'Emneth Early' AGM (syn. 'Early Victoria')
'Epicure' AGM (syn. 'Laxton's Epicure')
'Exeter Cross'
'Exquisite'
'Falstaff' AGM
'Fiesta' AGM
'Granny Smith'
'Greensleeves' AGM
'Grenadier' AGM
'Herefordshire Russet'
'Holstein' (triploid)
'James Grieve' AGM
'John Standish'
'Jonagold' AGM (triploid)
'Jonathan'
'Jumbo'
'Jupiter' AGM (triploid)
'Katy' (syn. 'Katja')
'Kidd's Orange Red' AGM
'King Russett' AGM
'Lane's Prince Albert' AGM
'Langley Pippin'
'Lord Hindlip'
'Malling Kent'
'Meridian'

'Merton Knave'
'Merton Prolific'
'Merton Russet'
'Miller's Seedling'
'Mutsu' (syn. 'Crispin') (triploid)
'Paradice Gold'
'Peasgood's Nonsuch' AGM
'Pinova'
'Polka' (syn. 'Trajan')
'Red Devil'
'Red Victoria'
'Redsleeves'
'Rubinette'
'Saint Cecilia'
'Saint Everard'
'Santana'
'Saturn'
'Scotch Dumpling'
'Scrumptious'
'Spartan'
'Stirling Castle'
'Sturmer Pippin'
'Sunset' AGM
'Taunton Cross'
'Tickled Pink'
'Tiedeman's Early Worcester'
'Tom Putt'
'Wagener'
'Waltz' (syn. 'Telamon')
'Winter Gem'
'Worcester Pearmain' AGM
'Wyke Pippin'

Group Four

'Annie Elizabeth'
'Ashmead's Kernel' AGM (triploid)
'Barnack Beauty'
'Cellini'
'Chiver's Delight'
'Claygate Pearmain' AGM
'Cornish Aromatic'
'Cornish Gillyflower'
'D'Arcy Spice'
'Delicious'
'Duke of Devonshire'
'Ellison's Orange' AGM
'Encore'
'Gala'
'George Carpenter'
'Gladstone'
'Gloster 69'
'Golden Delicious' AGM
'Golden Noble' AGM
'Herring's Pippin'
'Howgate Wonder'
'Ingrid Marie'
'Jester'
'King's Acre Pippin'
'Laxton's Superb'
'Laxton's Pearmain'
'Lord Derby'
'Merton Joy'
'Monarch'
'Orleans Reinette'
'Pixie'
'Sweet Society'
'Tydeman's Late Orange'
'Winston' AGM

Group Five

'Coronation'
'Gascoyne's Scarlet' (triploid)
'King of the Pippins' AGM
'Merton Beauty'
'Mother' AGM (syn. 'American Mother')
'Newton Wonder'
'Northern Spy'
'Royal Jubilee'
'Suntan' AGM (triploid)
'William Crump'

Group Six

'Bess Pool'
'Court Pendu Plat'
'Edward VII' AGM
'Laxton's Royalty'

Group Seven

'Crawley Beauty'

A bee nesting box. It is best to buy ones that are suitable for the local bee population.

Wall-trained fruit trees can be easily protected from spring frosts by homemade fleece-covered screens.

Pollinating insect populations can be maintained by keeping a wide range of flowering plants in the garden or orchard to provide nectar and pollen. Commercial orchards will often ensure that native flowering plants are allowed to flourish in their orchards in a move that will benefit both their crops and the environment. Avoiding pesticide usage is also essential. Pesticides are the last, rather than the first, resort in pest and disease control. If pesticides must be applied, late evening is the best time to do so when pollinating insects are less active.

Weather and Pollination

Apple blossom can be damaged by spring frosts, and even a brief night frost can wreak havoc. 'Frost pockets' in which cold air can accumulate are bad sites for planting fruit trees and bushes.

Later-flowering varieties (please refer to the flowering groups) are less susceptible to spring frost damage, but such is the capriciousness of the British weather that frosts can extend quite late into the season. Trained fruit can be protected from frost using horticultural fleece, which will give about two degrees of frost protection. For bush and standard trees, all is not lost by a frost occurring during flowering time as many trees will produce a secondary batch of blossom following the destruction of the first one by frost. Partial destruction of the blossom is not a disaster if all the flowers set fruit, and it will probably be necessary to carry out a lot of fruit thinning to avoid having too many small fruits and exhausting the tree.

Windy and cold weather can deter pollinating insects, particularly honeybees, which for all their laudable hard work are inclined to stay in the hive during cold weather. Solitary bees such as red mason bees are less affected by weather.

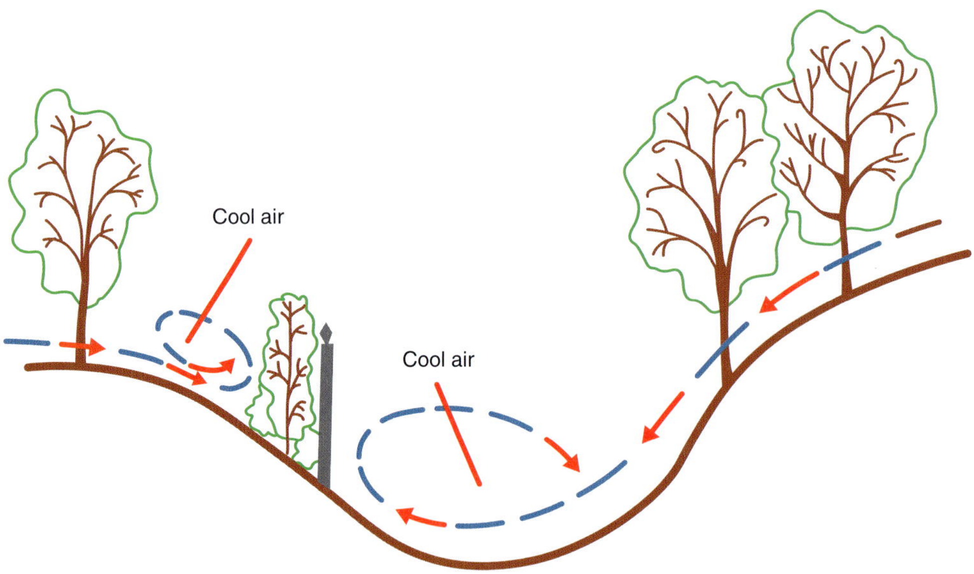

Cold air is heavier than warm air and its flow downwards can be obstructed by trees and walls. The cold air then accumulates in a hollow, which is known as a frost pocket.

Selected Varieties

With hundreds of varieties being offered by garden centres, specialist nurseries and online retailers, picking the right varieties can be daunting. Many garden writers will produce lists of what they say are the best varieties to grow, but this is a matter of personal choice. I have listed some remarkable apple varieties that may be worth considering, but with so much choice, it is hard to cater for everyone's taste. You may be surprised by the omission of Cox's Orange Pippin, but its susceptibility to disease, particularly scab, makes it very challenging to grow, especially without the use of chemical fungicides. Several varieties with Cox attributes are mentioned instead.

Dessert Varieties

Apple Ashmead's Kernel – a popular traditional variety with a fine aromatic flavour.

Apple Christmas Pippin – this modern variety was found as a chance seedling. It has Cox parentage.

Apple Discovery – a very popular eating apple with good disease resistance

Apple Honeycrisp – a very sweet dessert apple with excellent keeping qualities.

Apple Jupiter – a good substitute for Cox's Orange Pippin with a slightly more acidic flavour. This is a triploid variety so cannot act as a pollinator.

Apple Kidd's Orange Red – a Cox substitute from New Zealand with an excellent balance of sugar and acidity.

Apple Winter Gem – the fruits of this modern variety have an excellent flavour. Growth is vigorous so it is best grown on a dwarfing rootstock.

Apple Scrumptious – an outstanding modern variety for the amateur grower. It is attractive and very sweet, and is popular with children. It is self-fertile and comes into cropping early.

Apple Laxton's Superb – the attractive fruits have a Cox flavour. This fruit has a tendency to crop biennially and so careful pruning is required.

Adam's Pearmain

Adam's Pearmain is a heritage variety that has stood the test of time. The distinctive elongate fruits are crisp and juicy when eaten fresh and have a pleasant aromatic flavour and are good for juicing. The variety has good disease resistance and attractive spring flowers. This apple can be picked in late October and stored until March.

Ashmead's Kernel

The praises of this variety are sung by many apple enthusiasts. Described as having an intense flavour with a hint of pear drop and a good balance of acidity and sweetness, this variety is a good keeper. It is suitable for juicing or for making into cider. This apple is harvested in October and can be kept until February. Bear in mind that this variety is triploid.

Captain Kidd

This is a good variety for lovers of Cox's Orange Pippin who do not want the trouble of growing that variety. Captain Kidd is a variant of Kidd's Orange Red with improved colour. This New Zealand variety lost favour on account of the russeting of its skin rather than its delicious aromatic flesh. It will keep until January.

Christmas Pippin

Christmas Pippin was found as a chance seedling growing near an orchard in Somerset. The fruit has a distinctive Cox flavour, and probably this variety was one of its parents. Sweeter and less trouble than Cox, this apple will store until Christmas.

Crispin (Mutsu)

For lovers of Golden Delicious, Crispin is a much better choice of variety for growing in the UK. It comes from Japan but has found favour in Britain. The fruit is sweet and juicy, and the flavour improves with storage. Named Mutsu in Japan, the variety was named Crispin in the UK after a Women's Institute naming competition.

Discovery

Discovery is one of the best early apples and considered an improvement on its parent, Worcester Pearmain. The crisp, juicy flesh has a hint of strawberry, just like Worcester Pearmain. The variety is comparatively trouble-free and, like all early varieties, should be eaten straight from the tree in August.

Falstaff

Falstaff is a popular variety that was made by crossing Golden Delicious with James Grieve; it is another good variety for lovers of Cox. The attractive large apples are crisp and juicy with a good balance of sweetness and acidity. The variety is popular with commercial growers. It can store until March.

Fiesta

Fiesta is another good Cox substitute with crisp, aromatic, sweet and juicy flesh. This is a good variety for juicing. This variety is recommended for northern areas and is a firm favourite with commercial growers. It will store until January.

Gala

Gala is a variety from New Zealand and is the result of a cross between Kidd's Orange Red and Golden Delicious. The small apples are crisp and well flavoured and are often seen in supermarkets as improved colour varieties such as 'Royal Gala'. The fruit will store until January.

Herefordshire Russet

Hugh Ermen in Kent has bred many outstanding apple varieties, and Herefordshire Russet is one of them, created by crossing Cox's Orange Pippin with Golden Delicious. Credited with outstanding flavour and heavy cropping, this variety has won many taste trials and the small-to-medium fruits have an attractive amber russet skin. Disease resistance is good. The Cox parentage is evident in the rich aromatic flavour. This is an excellent choice for anybody who loves russets.

Honeycrisp

Honeycrisp is a good choice for lovers of sweet apples. The flesh is crisp and mild-flavoured but with plenty of sweetness. This is likely to find favour with children. This variety was bred in the USA to withstand cold winter conditions, and fruits can usually be stored in a garden shed until March in the UK.

Jupiter

Jupiter is a popular variety on account of its aromatic Cox flavour. It has Cox parentage but is more vigorous and easier to grow. Its vigour makes it a good variety for grafting on dwarfing rootstocks such as M9. The apples are large, sweet and juicy. This variety is triploid so it cannot function as a pollinator. It stores until January.

Kidds Orange Red

Raised in the early twentieth century from New Zealand, Kidds Orange Red has a sweet, Cox-like flavour. It is ready for picking in October, and can store until January. It belongs in pollination group 3.

Laxton's Superb

Laxton's Superb is a very popular late dessert apple grown by commercial growers both in the UK and the Netherlands. It has a good flavour and has Cox parentage. It is picked in October and can be kept until January. It is in pollination group 4.

Lord Lambourne

Lord Lambourne was the result of a cross between James Grieve and Worcester Pearmain. This aromatic apple is moderately sweet and has a firm, juicy flesh. There is a faint hint of strawberry in the flavour, a characteristic inherited from Worcester Pearmain. The apple is picked in September and will keep until November.

May Queen

May Queen is an attractive red apple with a distinctive flattish shape. The flesh is crisp and juicy and of particularly good flavour. This outstanding variety lost favour with commercial growers on account of its tendency to have some russeting, but if that is not an issue, it is a good choice. The apple should keep until March or even later.

Pitmaston Pineapple

Pitmaston Pineapple is a very distinctive apple. It is a small golden russet with an assortment of flavours that include pineapple, honey and musk. The flavour will vary from one season to another. Growth is moderate, so it is a good variety if space is restricted.

Ribston Pippin

Ribston Pippin is famed for being a parent of Cox's Orange Pippin. The pale yellow flesh is flavoursome, crisp, and slightly more acidic than Cox. The fruit can store until January, and makes a particularly good juice, rich in vitamin C. Being a triploid, this variety is not suitable as a pollinator.

Saturn

Saturn is a variety for lovers of sweet apples. Like many modern varieties, it is crisp, sweet and juicy but rather mild. It is a reliable cropper and self-fertile, and has good disease resistance; it stores until February.

Scrumptious

Scrumptious is another variety bred by Hugh Ermen that is worthy of mention for many reasons. The bright red fruits are crisp and juicy and absolutely delicious. The variety is precocious – it comes into cropping early – and it is disease-resistant and self-fertile. In addition, the blossoms show a good degree of frost resistance. Its only slight drawback is that it is not heavy cropping so it will appeal more to the amateur rather than the professional grower.

Sunset

The variety Sunset was found from a seedling of Cox's Orange Pippin and has inherited much of the flavour from its parent. However, it is immeasurably easier to grow on account of its disease resistance and reliable cropping. Growth is moderate, so it is a useful variety for a restricted space. It stores until December.

Winter Gem

Winter Gem is another variety bred by Hugh Ermen and is noted for its excellent flavour. The fruits are flushed pink and have an excellent balance of sugar and acidity. Growth is vigorous and is best controlled using a dwarfing rootstock. A good keeper, the fruits can store until March.

Culinary (Cooking) Varieties

Apple Arthur Turner – this culinary apple has outstandingly beautiful blossom for which it has received an Award of Garden Merit (AGM) from the Royal Horticultural Society.

Apple Bramley's Seedling – the most popular cooking apple, excellent for sauces, pies and juice. The fruits sweeten on storage and the apple can be eaten uncooked in spring.

Apple Bountiful – a good substitute variety for Bramley's Seedling that is more compact. It is mildew resistant.

Apple Howgate Wonder – a very large culinary apple that can win prizes at village shows. It retains its shape when cooked and so is good for baking (baked apples).

Arthur Turner

Quite apart from its excellence as a cooking apple, this variety has had recognition for its attractive pink blossoms, for which it has received an award of merit from the Royal Horticultural Society. The apples bake well, and also make a well-flavoured purée that requires little sweetening. An additional bonus is the variety's disease resistance. It stores until November.

Bountiful

The variety Bountiful ripens earlier than Bramley. It keeps its shape when cooked, and so is useful as a pie topping and for other apple desserts. When cooked, the flesh is quite sweet; the apples may also be eaten fresh by lovers of sharp apples. Disease resistance is good, and the fruits can be picked in September and stored until November.

Bramley's Seedling and Bramley 20

No other cooking apple is held in the same esteem as Bramley's Seedling. Its fame is truly international, and enthusiasts for this variety come from as far afield as North America and Japan. The original Bramley's Seedling was grown from a pip in 1809 by Mary Ann Brailsford in her Nottinghamshire garden. In 1856, the nurseryman Henry Merryweather asked the then owner of the tree, Matthew Bramley, if he could take scions from the tree to propagate it. Bramley agreed, provided that the variety was called Bramley's Seedling, a rather disingenuous act that robbed Mary Ann Brailsford of her rightful fame. The sharp acidic flavour and cooking quality is lauded by cooks, and the juice is outstanding, with a refreshing taste. The fruits sweeten on storage and can be eaten fresh in spring or in winter salads. The variety will store until March or even later.

For all its attributes, Bramley has one possible limitation – its vigour. Like many triploid varieties, it makes vigorous growth, which may pose problems for small gardens. The variety Bramley 20 has all the virtues of Bramley's Seedling, but makes 20 per cent less growth. The alternative to selecting Bramley 20 is to have Bramley's Seedling on a dwarfing rootstock. Bramley, like all triploids, is an ineffective pollinator.

Edward VII

Edward VII is a late-flowering variety and so is useful for areas troubled by spring frosts. The apples cook to a fine purée. The variety has good scab resistance; it also has good keeping qualities and will store until March.

Howgate Wonder

This variety produces impressive large apples with a red flush and excellent cooking qualities; the apple keeps its shape when baked. Like many cooking varieties, it will sweeten on storage and can be eaten fresh after Christmas. The tree can make vigorous growth, so it is best on a dwarfing rootstock. The variety has good disease resistance, and the fruit can be stored until March.

Lanes Prince Albert

Lanes Prince Albert is a suitable alternative to Bramley's Seedling for confined spaces as it makes compact growth. Being spur-bearing, it is also more suitable for cordon or espalier growing than Bramley's Seedling. The green fruits are flushed pink and can cook to a fine purée. The variety has good keeping qualities and should store until March.

Reverend W. Wilks

Reverend W. Wilks is an outstanding early cooking variety that is considered self-fertile. Growth is moderate, so it is an excellent choice for small gardens. When cooked the apples need little additional sugar. It is not a good keeper but has good disease resistance.

Trinity

Trinity is an unusual cooking variety in several ways. The relatively small fruits have a dark red skin, and the flesh is pink. The fruits do not have to be peeled as the skin dissolves during cooking. The fruit can be picked in August and stored until September.

Dual-purpose Varieties

Apple Bardsey – a remarkable dual-purpose apple that is very disease-resistant.

Apple Charles Ross – an excellent dual-purpose apple with the aromatic qualities of Cox. It is also useful for juicing.

Apple Bloody Ploughman – an attractive dual-purpose apple with a sinister past.

Apple James Grieve – an excellent dual-purpose apple that remains popular.

Bardsey

This apple was found growing wild on Bardsey Island off the west Welsh coast. The nurseryman Ian Sturrock took the fruits to the National Fruit Collection in Brogdale, Kent, where it was confirmed that it was an unknown variety; it was named after the island where it was found. The attractive apples have a pink flush, lemon scent and refreshing flavour. The fruit cooks to a sweet purée, or can be eaten fresh. The disease resistance of this variety is remarkable, as is its ability to grow in difficult conditions. Its main limitation is that it will not store.

Blenheim Orange

Blenheim Orange is mainly known as a dessert apple, but it does have good cooking qualities as well. The attractive yellow apples have an orange flush with red stripes. The flesh is aromatic with a sweet, nutty flavour. When cooked, the fruits retain their shape, flavour and colour. This apple is valued by heritage apple enthusiasts. The fruit is picked in October and can store until January. Being triploid, this variety is an ineffective pollinator.

Bloody Ploughman

The variety Bloody Ploughman has a sinister story concerning its origins. It is rumoured that this apple arose from the grave of an unfortunate ploughman who was shot in the act of stealing apples from the Megginch estate in Scotland. His wife was given the apples, but threw them away in disgust. One of the seedlings from the apples was rescued by another worker and bore attractive dark red fruits that were considered worthy of cultivation. This variety is suitable for eating fresh for lovers of sharp apples, or for cooking. The apples are picked in September and can be stored until November. This variety has good disease resistance.

Charles Ross

Charles Ross is a popular and outstanding apple for eating fresh, and is also good for baking. It is suitable for growing in northern areas. The attractive greenish-yellow fruits have an orange flush and red stripes. The flesh is sweet and juicy. To add to its versatility, this apple is great for juicing as well. It has good disease resistance. There is a colour variant of this variety called 'Red Charles Ross'.

Cobra

This modern apple comes from crossing two distinguished heritage varieties: Bramley's Seedling and Cox's Orange Pippin. Unsurprisingly it makes an outstanding dual-purpose apple. The name derives from the first two letters of the names of the parent varieties. This is another introduction by Hugh Ermen of Kent. The apples are picked in September when they have a sharp, tart taste for cooking, but after a period of storage they will become sweeter for eating fresh. The variety has good disease resistance.

James Grieve

James Grieve is a popular variety that has stood the test of time and is self-fertile. The fruits have a red flush, and the creamy-white flesh is juicy. It is a reliable cropper and is still grown commercially. There is a colour variant of this variety called 'Red James Grieve'. Fruits are best picked underripe for cooking, but should be allowed to ripen fully on the tree for eating fresh. Apples are picked in September and will store for a month.

Jumbo

Jumbo is a large apple with an acidic aromatic flavour; it bakes well, and retains its shape when cooked. The pale skin is flushed and striped red. The fruits are ready in September and can be stored until March. This is another Ermen introduction. Like many large apples, this variety is triploid.

Orléans Reinette

The apple Orléans Reinette is very popular in France. It has been likened to a Blenheim Orange with sweet, nutty, firm flesh. For cooking purposes it is best picked and cooked underripe and left to ripen on the tree for eating fresh. The fruit will store until January. This is a relatively trouble-free variety.

Rootstocks

As mentioned previously, rootstocks provide a convenient means of propagation and help to moderate shoot growth. Apples are notoriously difficult to root from cuttings, and without the moderating effect of many rootstocks they would make trees that are too tall to manage properly and fit into small gardens. Before named rootstocks were developed, apples would be grafted on to crab-apple seedlings. The nursery would determine the vigour of the seedling to get the desired effects. In the early twentieth century the East Malling Research Station researched into producing rootstocks that had known characteristics and could be vegetatively propagated. The results were outstandingly successful, and one of the results of this research, the apple rootstock M9, is the most widely grown apple rootstock in the world.

Rootstocks were assessed in terms of vigour but also according to their ability to grow in difficult soil and their tolerance of waterlogging, and pest and disease resistance were also considered. As apple growing is a truly pan-global enterprise, other rootstock development work has continued in the United States, Poland, Russia, and other countries. In Eastern Europe tolerance of cold winter temperatures is important, while in the United States resistance to the devastating bacterial disease fireblight is an important factor.

In Britain, most apple rootstocks are prefixed with an M, indicating their origin from the East Malling Research Station. What may be seen as confusing is that there is no apparent correlation between the allocated number and the vigour of the rootstock. For example, the rootstock M27 is extremely dwarfing, M9 is slightly more vigorous, and M26 is more vigorous than M9. MM106 (MM stands for Malling Merton) is more vigorous than M26 and is the most common rootstock for apple trees grown for amateur gardeners. MM111 makes a more vigorous tree than MM106.

Rootstocks being grown at a nursery using the stool bed method.

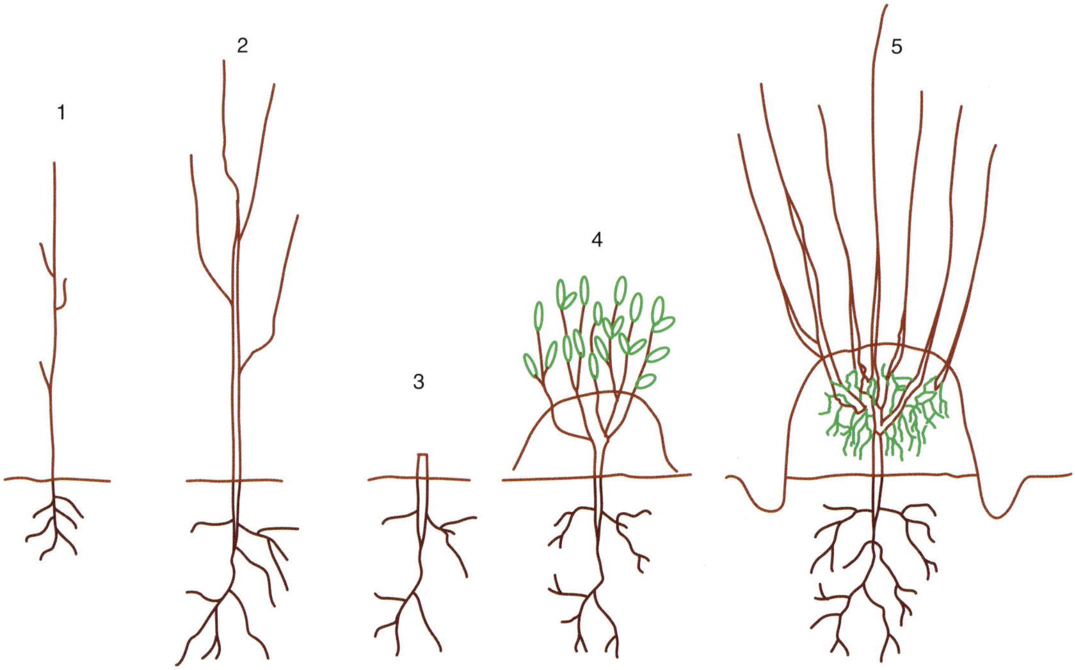

Mound layering:
Step 1: The rootstock is planted.
Step 2: The rootstock is allowed to grow.
Step 3: The rootstock is pruned back hard.
Step 4: Soil is mounded round the base of the rootstock.
Step 5: The branches covered by soil take root and are detached in winter to grow as independent plants.

M25 is used primarily for farm orchards that may have to support livestock.

Rootstocks are usually propagated by mound layering, in which a rootstock is planted and then cut back, and as new growth develops, it is partially covered by soil or sawdust in a process similar to earthing up potatoes. Covering the base of the emerging shoots encourages the development of roots arising directly from the stems (adventitious roots). At the end of the growing season, the shoots are removed with their adventitious roots attached and these can be grown independently.

M27 (Extremely Dwarfing)

Trees usually grow to 1.2–1.5m (4–5ft) in height. Trees grown on this rootstock are often called 'patio trees' as they are considered small enough to grow in pots on patios. The advantage of this rootstock is that it enables many easily manageable trees to be grown in a relatively small area. If grown in an orchard, the plant spacings in the rows should be 1.2–1.5m (4–5ft) with the rows spaced 1.8m (6ft) apart. If grown in pots, a loam-based growing medium is ideal. Alternatively the trees can be grown in a fertile soil. Trees grown on this rootstock need permanent staking.

M9 (Dwarfing)

Trees normally grow to 1.8–2.4m (6–8ft) in height. M9 is the world's most popular apple rootstock. An interesting feature of this rootstock is that fruits tend to be larger than on other rootstocks. Trees on this rootstock need a good soil, or can be grown in large containers with a loam-based growing medium. Trees should be spaced 2.4 to 3m (8 to 10ft) apart, with rows spaced 3.6m (12ft) apart. Trees require permanent staking.

M26 (Dwarfing)

Trees on this rootstock are more vigorous than those on M9, growing between 2.4 and 3m (8 and 10ft) in height. This rootstock is less fussy about soil than M9, and is happy on average soils. It is a popular rootstock with amateurs. Possible disadvantages include its susceptibility to woolly aphid and possibly collar rot. Although not a major concern in the UK, M26 is reputed to have poor resistance to fireblight. Trees should be planted 3.6m (12ft) apart in rows, and the rows should be spaced 4.5m (15ft) apart. Trees need permanent staking.

MM106 (intermediate)

Trees normally grow between 3 and 4m (10 and 13ft) in height. This is the most popular rootstock for amateur growers in the UK, and will grow happily in a range of different soils. Trees should be spaced at least 3.6m (12ft) apart, with a minimum of 4.5m (15ft) between rows. They will need staking for the first three years.

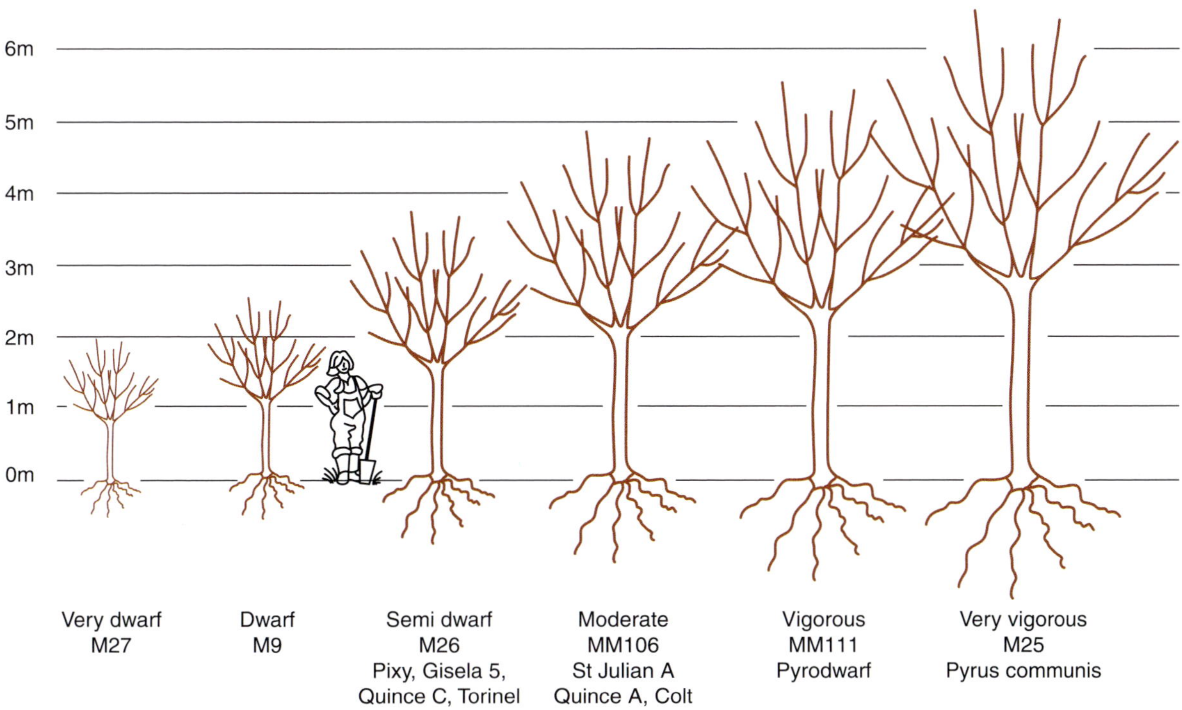

Rootstock vigour chart.

MM111 (Vigorous)

Trees normally grow between 4 and 4.5m (13 and 15ft) in height, which is too large for many gardens; however, this can be useful where larger trees are required, such as in community orchards. Apart from issues of manageability, trees on vigorous rootstocks may take up to five years to come into bearing. Trees should be given a minimum spacing of 4.5m (15ft), and rows should be spaced at least 6m (20ft) apart. Trees may need staking for the first three years.

M25 (Very Vigorous)

This rootstock produces trees between 4.5 and 6m (15 and 20ft) in height. It is therefore limited to situations where very large trees are required that may be difficult to manage without the use of ladders. Trees should have a minimum spacing of 6m (20ft), and will need only initial staking.

Although I have explained the value of rootstocks in apple-tree propagation and training, there are some advocates of growing apples on their own roots. The possible advantages of trees on their own roots are the avoidance of graft incompatibility, and improved tree health and fruit quality. Experiments using trees on their own roots and comparing them with grafted trees are not conclusive and more work needs to be done. Instead of using rootstocks to moderate vigour, trees on their own roots are moderated by reducing the availability of plant nutrients such as nitrogen, practising summer rather than winter pruning, and tying down branches.

Diseases, Disorders and Pests

There are many pests, diseases and disorders of apples, and to list them all would make growing apples appear very daunting and cause undue alarm. I have highlighted the main ones, looking at their symptoms and control methods. Many older books will talk at length about chemical control, but this has rapidly lost favour with horticulturists. Many insecticides were developed in the last century as a result of researching and developing chemical weapons. However, the excessive use of pesticides led to environmental damage, as described by Rachel Carson in her iconic book *Silent Spring*, published in 1962.

In addition to the danger posed to humans, animals and the environment, an additional and important reason for the decline in chemical control for pests and diseases is the development of natural resistance to chemical pesticides, making them ineffective. Chemicals are still used to control pests and diseases of fruit, but they are used as the last resort, rather than the first. Cultural methods such as the selection of resistant varieties, pruning, nutrition and irrigation take precedence over chemical control. Encouraging the natural enemies of pests such as lacewings, hoverflies and ladybirds can provide environmentally friendly control strategies for many pests, particularly aphids.

For decades, chemical control gave growers a cheap and convenient method of eliminating many pests, but at great environmental cost. Modern methods of pest and disease control no longer adopt a zero-tolerance approach. Some pests, such as winter moth and capsid bugs, cause little damage when the pest population is low, and control methods are only used when it exceeds a threshold of acceptability.

The term 'pesticide' is a generic one and covers both insecticides and fungicides. Some products are classified as for professional use only, and must be used only by people who hold an appropriate qualification in the storage and application of pesticides. Most horticultural colleges and a variety of private training providers will run pesticide courses throughout the year. It is unlawful for unqualified people to purchase and apply professional pesticides. In addition, professional pesticides must be stored in an approved chemical store, the user must use the specified personal protective equipment (PPE), and must keep appropriate records of pesticide use.

Both amateur and professional users of pesticides must only use approved chemicals. Approval for a pesticide may be withdrawn for a variety of reasons, making its use after a specified time unlawful. Products or substances that are not approved for use as a pesticide cannot be used: this includes the home remedies often advocated by 'experts' such as vinegar, washing-up liquid, and concoctions made by boiling cigarette butts.

Amateur gardeners must follow the safety instructions on the packaging of the pesticide, including how the product is to be used. Fruit plants can only be sprayed with products authorised for use on edibles.

Diseases

Scab

Apple scab is a potentially serious and common fungal disease of apples and causes the biggest headache to commercial growers. It is caused by the fungus Venturia inaequalis, and apart from apples can be seen on other members of the rose family such as Cotoneaster and Pyracantha. A closely related fungus, Venturia pyrina, is the cause of scab disease in pears. The symptoms of this disease are olive-green spots on the foliage: these have a velvety feel, and darken as the fungus releases its airborne spores. Twigs can become infected, showing blistering. Fruits become covered in black and brown spots, which can then develop cracks. Scab-infected fruits are edible, but their appearance makes them unmarketable for commercial growers. Cracked fruits will not store.

The best method of minimising apple scab is to select varieties with natural resistance to this disease. Many modern varieties such as Scrumptious have good scab resistance, as do some heritage varieties such as Ashmead's Kernel. Susceptibility to scab has made the variety Cox's Orange Pippin difficult to grow, especially without the use of fungicides.

Raking up and disposing of fallen leaves in autumn will remove the major source of infection, as will pruning out blistered wood. Currently there are no fungicides approved for scab control on apples for amateur use.

Powdery Mildew

Powdery mildew is commonly seen on apples but is usually less damaging than apple scab. It is a fungal disease caused by the fungus Podosphaera leucotricha. Apple powdery mildew is sometimes seen on pears and quinces, but powdery mildews are host specific so will not spread from Michaelmas daisies to apples, or vice versa. The main symptoms are white powdery patches on leaves and stems. As with all fungal pathogens, infection will reduce plant vigour and cropping potential. Cutting out congested growth

Apple scab is a potentially serious fungal disease of apples. Some varieties show good resistance to this disease.

Powdery mildew is a common disease that can be partially controlled by correct pruning.

will improve air circulation in the plant as well as allowing the entry of light to ripen the fruit. Powdery mildew can overwinter on fallen leaves, so raking these up is an important form of control. Apple varieties will vary in their mildew resistance, and Cox's Orange Pippin is particularly prone to this disease, but it is better to select varieties with natural resistance to scab as this is the more difficult disease to control.

Products based on natural plant oils are proving promising in the battle against powdery mildew. These products use a physical rather than chemical method to control mildew. They may also control growth stimulants and help to control aphids, and so perform a variety of useful functions.

Note that overfeeding with nitrogenous fertilisers can favour powdery mildews by promoting soft, lush growth that is easily infected.

Canker

Apple canker is a disease caused by the fungus Neonectria ditissima. This pathogen has a wide host range including pears, maples and birch, but apple is the commonest host. The fungus usually gains entry via pruning cuts, blisters caused by scab, or wounds caused by breaking. The disease is most easily seen in winter, in round or oval patches of sunken bark. Thin branches usually die back within a year, but cankers on thicker branches may last several years. The tree fights infection by trying to grow over the canker, causing a swelling around its edge. In some cases the tree can grow over the canker, but usually the canker wins, and the branch dies back beyond the point of infection. The disease is more common in wet areas and on acid soils. Some varieties are more susceptible to this disease, such as Cox's Orange Pippin and James Grieve.

The only effective treatment is to cut out the cankers, burn or dispose of infected wood, and treat the surfaces of pruning cuts with a proprietary wound paint. The pruning saw should be cleaned with a suitable sterilant such as methylated spirits after each canker has been removed to avoid spreading infection.

Brown Rot

Brown rot is a common disease caused by the fungi Monilinia laxa and Monolinia fructigena in which fruits rot and turn brown, often starting from puncture wounds. This disease can affect other fruits, particularly plums. Puncture wounds are often caused by birds or codling moths. The fungi can also cause blossoms and foliage to wilt in spring. In some cases the rotten fruits fall, in others they become mummified and stay on the tree.

The main methods of control include the removal of infected spurs and rotten fruits, and discouraging bird attacks by netting or the use of scarers.

Apple canker is a fungal disease that can be controlled by pruning out the affected growths.

Brown rot is caused by two different fungal pathogens and is best controlled by the removal of affected spurs.

Collar and Crown Rot

Collar and crown rot are similar diseases, both caused by the pathogen Phytophthora cactorum, which is a fungus-like organism and a near relative of the pathogen that causes potato blight. Both diseases are associated with waterlogged soils. Collar rot is a disease that affects the area around the graft union, and is mainly seen on older trees aged ten years or more; Cox's Orange Pippin is particularly susceptible to this disease. Crown rot is a disease of the rootstock and is usually seen in young trees that are establishing themselves.

Collar rot is seldom controllable, and the best course of action is to remove the affected tree and improve soil drainage before replanting. The rootstock MM106 shows good resistance to collar rot. Crown rot may be treatable by the removal of infected tissue, but it is indicative of poor soil conditions that cannot be addressed without the removal of the affected trees and improving soil drainage.

Virus Diseases

There are several virus diseases of apples that cause a reduction of vigour and reduced cropping, often with a severe reduction in fruit quality. Apple mosaic virus causes random mottling of the foliage and poor yields. Apple star crack virus can cause a dramatic reduction in fruit size and a characteristic cracking of the fruits. Other viruses are difficult to identify as there are no visible symptoms, but growth and yield can be badly affected. It is not possible to remove virus infection from a tree. If yields remain acceptable the tree can be left in place, but graft wood should never be taken from an infected tree.

Physiological Disorders

Physiological disorders cannot be attributed to a pest or a disease, and are usually caused by environmental conditions such as frost and waterlogging, or nutrient deficiencies. They may be alleviated by better choice of planting site, the use of resilient varieties, and careful nutrition. One disorder that can cause problems in apples is 'bitter pit'. This is associated with low levels of calcium in the fruit caused by lack of moisture in the soil, leading to reduced mobility of the nutrient in the plant. It is particularly common following hot, dry summers. This disorder is characterised by small sunken pits on the surface of the fruit, and the fruit flesh is discoloured and dry. In severe cases the spots are scattered throughout the flesh, which develops an unpleasant, bitter taste.

Bitter pit can occur in calcium-rich soils such as chalky ones, and the remedy is to irrigate, or to apply a calcium nitrate solution directly to the foliage using a sprayer. Mulching trees will help to conserve water, and a light summer pruning will reduce vigour and help to direct calcium to the fruit. The symptoms can appear from midsummer onwards, and in some cases only develop after the fruit has been harvested. The incidence of bitter pit can be reduced by using a spray made by dissolving 10g of calcium nitrate per litre of water, and applying it until it starts to run off the foliage.

There is some varietal difference for susceptibility to bitter pit; for example, Cox's Orange Pippin and Bramley's Seedling are prone to the disease, whereas Gala and Jonathon appear immune.

Pests

Codling Moth

Codling moth is a common pest of apples and is easily identified by the damage caused by the caterpillars eating away at the inside of the fruit and leaving a distinctive exit hole. The pest is occasionally found in quinces and walnuts. Sometimes the caterpillar is found in the fruits, along with copious amounts of its excrement (frass). Fruits tend to ripen and drop prematurely. Commercial orchards can suffer serious loss of fruit and must adopt several control measures; amateur growers can usually afford to be more tolerant of this pest.

Pheromone traps are commonly used as part of a control strategy. They act by releasing a small amount of a sex attractant emitted by female moths to attract males. Males are drawn to the traps and trapped by an adhesive sheet. Pheromone traps do not give complete control of codling moth. In commercial orchards, the traps are analysed, and the numbers of trapped moths monitored to see if the population of the pest warrants chemical control methods. Traps designed for monitoring apple codling moth will not work for plum codling moth and vice versa as they are different species. In gardens, the traps may reduce the moth population to a tolerable level.

Natural predation of codling moth eggs by birds such as blue tits and ground beetles can also reduce populations of the pest. Additional biological control using nematodes (eelworms) can be effective. These are applied in late summer to the trunk and branches of the tree after the caterpillars have emerged. Raking leaves and debris from around the base of the tree will help to remove overwintering caterpillars.

If large populations of codling moths are found in traps, there may be some justification for using an approved pesticide. This is usually applied around the third week in June. It is essential that the pesticide is approved for control of codling moth; if in doubt, contact the manufacturers for advice. Although caterpillars will often crawl from the ground on to the trunk and branches, grease bands will provide only limited control of this pest.

Apple Sawfly

The pest 'apple sawfly' is as common as codling moth. Small populations can be beneficial as they can help to thin out fruitlets, leading to increased fruit size and quality. The pest is first seen in late May to June with obvious holes in the fruitlets, and with the excrement of the caterpillars (frass) often protruding from the exit hole. Caterpillars can move from one fruitlet to another, so the removal of damaged fruitlets will stop others being attacked. Most attacked fruitlets will fall from the tree during the 'June drop' period. Fruits with minimal damage may remain on the tree and will have a noticeable ribbon-like scar. Once they have finished feeding, caterpillars drop to the ground and pupate the following spring. Adults visit the trees during blossom time and lay their eggs at the base of the flowers.

Apart from the removal of damaged fruits, control measures include the encouragement of natural predators such as birds; chemical control with an approved pesticide should be used as a last resort. If chemical control is used, sprays are applied when at least 80 per cent of the petals have fallen from the tree and pollination has finished.

Aphids

Aphids can be serious pests, mainly because they can reproduce asexually for much of the growing season. In summer all female populations give birth to pregnant nymphs by the process of parthenogenesis. Aphids feed by sucking sap selectively, feeding on proteins and rejecting sugars, which fall on to lower foliage and result in 'sooty' moulds. Large populations of a pest will attract predators and so biological control methods are useful for keeping the populations of this pest in check. The sugar secreted by aphids is eaten by ants, which will protect aphid colonies from predators such as ladybirds. The presence of ants moving up the trunk of the tree is a sign that aphids are feeding.

There are three main aphid species that attack apples, namely the rosy, green and woolly aphid. They are most active in early summer and are found in dense colonies on young shoots. The leaves of these shoots are often curled inwards, making the pests difficult to reach with chemical sprays. In fact aphids can build up resistance to chemical pesticides very rapidly, so apart from the environmental considerations, chemical control may be ineffective in many cases. Some aphid control products contain surfactants as well as a growth stimulator and may give better control, but it is essential to contact the pest when using these sprays and that is not always easy. Encouraging natural predators such as birds, lacewings, hoverflies and ladybirds is important when keeping aphids in check.

Aphids feeding on an apple tree. They can reproduce very quickly and become a serious pest. Fortunately they have many natural predators.

Woolly Aphid

The woolly aphid is a distinctive pest and is found on both fruiting and ornamental varieties of apple, and also on Pyracantha and Cotoneaster. The dark aphids are covered by a fluffy white waxy material. In spring, the aphids are usually clustered round pruning cuts, but move to younger shoots later. Lumpy growths appear on stems because of the aphids feeding. These growths may split following frosts, which provides entry points for infection by apple canker. After feeding in summer, the aphids overwinter in bark crevices until spring, when they resume feeding. During winter, the aphids do not produce the white, waxy coating. Woolly aphids may be more common on trees planted on the rootstock M26, which is susceptible to this pest.

The waxy coating on woolly aphids makes them resistant to chemical sprays.

Control of this pest by chemical methods is difficult. The waxy coating repels chemical sprays, and the aphids hide deep in bark crevices in winter, making it difficult to reach them with winter washes. Systemic sprays that can enter the plant and poison the sap are not available to amateur gardeners for edible crops.

Winter Moth

There are several species of winter moth. They lay their eggs in the branches of apple trees, and these eggs hatch and the resulting caterpillars feed on foliage and fruitlets. Eggs are laid by wingless females that crawl up the tree to lay their eggs after mating. These pests seldom do enough damage to warrant control measures, and the caterpillars are an important food source for birds such as blue tits. If this pest is getting out of control, grease bands can be attached to the trunk during winter to trap the females before they are able to reach the branches to lay their eggs.

Capsid Bugs

These beetle-like insects are commonly seen on fruit trees and feed on foliage, causing small, brown-edged holes in the leaves and small corky 'outgrowths' on fruits. Commercial growers concerned about the appearance of their fruit take control measures, but as capsid damage affects neither the eating nor storage qualities of the affected apples, control is seldom necessary for amateurs.

Capsid bug damage on apple. The corky outgrowths on the fruit are typical symptoms of this pest.

Birds

Birds can be a troublesome pest and will often take small pecks out of ripening fruit, rendering it useless. Peck holes made by birds may then become colonised by wasps as they seek sugar. In small orchards, decoy raptors may provide some control, but birds soon become wise to the fact that the decoy is not a real predator and resume attacks after a short while. It is best to set up the decoy just as the fruit is ripening so the birds do not have time to become accustomed to it. Objects such as CDs hung from strings above the trees may also have some deterrent effect. Small trees may be netted, but this is very time-consuming.

Bullfinches can damage fruit trees by eating the fruit buds in spring. King Henry VIII of England, who had a keen interest in fruit growing, denounced the 'criminal damage' caused by these birds and an act of parliament was passed in which a penny bounty was paid for every bullfinch killed. However, even though it was once considered a serious pest of orchards, the UK population of this beautiful bird has declined rapidly in recent decades, and this has caused concern amongst environmentalists. Control methods including trapping and shooting are illegal, apart from instances when professional growers can make a case for control if experiencing severe bullfinch damage. It may be possible to lure bullfinches away from trees by keeping feeders well supplied with seeds; otherwise the loss of a few fruit buds might be considered a contribution to helping conserve a beautiful and increasingly rare bird.

Pruning and Training

With so much potentially confusing information concerning the pruning and training of fruit trees, I shall endeavour to simplify the subject. It is worth considering the reasons why we prune before getting out the pruning saw, secateurs and loppers. The productive capacity of a tree can be reduced by thoughtless pruning.

It is important to be able to assess the growth that the tree has made in terms of vigour, placement of branches, incidence of pests and diseases, and the relative amount of fruit and growth buds. Blindly following pruning diagrams without 'reading' the tree is seldom the best approach.

Reasons for Pruning

- To restrict the size of the tree to keep it to a manageable size and within its allocated space.
- To maintain a balance between old and new wood.
- To achieve optimal cropping.
- To control pests and diseases.
- To minimise biennial bearing.
- To improve fruit quality.
- To avoid broken branches through overcropping.
- To improve the appearance of the tree.
- To remove sucker growth from rootstocks.

Birds can be troublesome pests of top fruit by making small pecks in ripe fruits that rapidly deteriorate.

Broken branches caused by overcropping can rapidly become infected; prompt removal is essential.

Fruit buds (pictured here) are swollen and grow out from the stem; growth buds are flattened.

Like all woody plants, an apple tree aims to make strong, upright growth so that it can compete with other plants to get its foliage to reach the light. Strong, upright growth is not very productive in terms of bearing fruit, which is mainly borne on horizontal or near horizontal branches. With a few notable exceptions, most apple varieties do not produce fruit buds on new growth. These are usually produced on wood that is two years old or older. Fruit buds are easily distinguished from growth buds as they are larger and grow out from the stem. Growth buds are small and flat. Being able to distinguish between fruit and growth buds is important for effective pruning. Having the right proportion of each is necessary to maintain cropping and the ability to produce new growth that will bear future crops. As wood on apple trees becomes older, its ability to produce quality fruit declines, hence the need to replace old wood with new growth to maintain optimal cropping.

The tips of upward-growing branches produce hormones that suppress the growth of lower buds. This is to encourage the development of strong upward growth for the foliage to reach the light. The removal of the uppermost (apical) bud stops the suppression of lateral growth, so pruning branch tips will encourage side growth.

When assessing the pruning requirements of a tree, it is necessary to ascertain its vigour. New growth is easy to spot, as it is usually unbranched and only has growth rather than fruit buds. At the base of new growth, a 'girdle scar' is easily identified. A young tree should make vigorous growth during its formative years, though excessive growth may be the result of too hard winter pruning and could be at the expense of fruit production. Lack of vigour may be the result of insufficient pruning and will ultimately result in poor cropping or fruit quality.

Winter pruning usually increases the vigour of a tree, while summer pruning has the reverse effect. Winter pruning is usually carried out on bush and standard trees, and has the advantage of being an operation that can be carried out during a quieter period of the year for horticultural operations; also the lack of foliage means that the branch framework is easier to see. Branches without the weight of foliage are easier to remove during the dormant period.

Espaliers, cordons and fans are summer pruned to restrict their vigour. Summer pruning robs the tree of nutrients stored in the leaves and stems, thereby reducing vigour and favouring the formation of fruit buds in preference to growth buds.

The pruning of young trees aims to establish the basic shape and branch framework. This is called formative pruning. After the basic shape has been achieved by formative pruning, a system of pruning is used to maintain the balance of old and new wood and promote optimal cropping. This is called maintenance pruning. The pruning of neglected trees to get them back into shape and optimal production is called regenerative pruning.

There are many tree forms that are used to grow apples, and for the sake of brevity I will discuss the open-centre forms for bush and standard trees, espalier, cordon and stepover types. The pruning of commercial tree forms such as spindle bushes, dwarf pyramids and vertical cordons is explained on specialist websites.

Formative Pruning of Open-Centre Bush and Standard Trees

Formative pruning techniques will vary according to the specification of the tree. Unfeathered maiden trees (whips) consist of one unbranched shoot arising from the graft union. Feathered maidens have side shoots developing from the main stem, and these are used to make the main (scaffold) branches.

For a feathered whip, the main stem should be cut just above a wide-angled shoot at an approximate height of 75cm (30in). There should be three to five evenly spaced shoots below this cut. These shoots are pruned hard by about two-thirds to an outward-facing bud. These shoots will form the main scaffold branches, and the remaining shoots should be cut out.

For an unfeathered maiden, the main shoot should be pruned to about the same height just above four growth buds that will be encouraged to grow because of pruning out the apical bud. Once these shoots have grown, the resultant tree is pruned in the same way as a feathered maiden.

To make a standard or half-standard tree, the main stem should be allowed to grow to a greater height before cutting back. This is usually possible because trees to be grown as standards or half-standards are grown on more vigorous rootstocks than those used for bush trees, and consequently make more vigorous growth. For a half-standard, the leading shoot should be pruned at a height of about 1.2m (4ft), while for a standard tree, this height should be increased to about 1.8m (6ft). If there is insufficient growth on the main shoot, it should be tipped back by a third to encourage extension growth in the following season. The main branches are pruned in the same way as those on bush trees.

The following year, the main branches are cut back by a third of their previous season's growth. Side growths from these branches are left unpruned unless they are growing inwards or rub or cross with other growth. Strong upward growths are also removed as these are usually unproductive.

Many bush trees bought from a garden centre or nursery require the main branches to be cut back to encourage the formation of side shoots.

Maintenance Pruning

Once the tree has achieved its correct shape through formative pruning, maintenance pruning aims to encourage optimal productivity by maintaining the correct balance between mature and new growth, and allowing light and air to penetrate the canopy of the tree. There are several pruning systems that are used for maintenance pruning.

Spur pruning involves the hard pruning of side growths (laterals) to form 'spurs' that carry the fruit. The new growth on leading shoots is pruned back by about a third. This is a simple system and works well with the majority of apple varieties that are 'spur bearers'. The main disadvantage of spur pruning is that it tends to remove new growth at the expense of achieving the correct balance of new and older wood. An additional problem arises with the so-called 'tip-bearing' apple varieties.

Whereas most apples varieties produce fruit buds on wood that is two years old or older, tip bearers produce fruit buds at the end of one-year-old growth. Cutting back new growth in winter will remove the fruit buds from tip-bearing trees, preventing cropping. The early apple variety 'Irish Peach' is a typical tip bearer. To complicate the issue further, some varieties are described as 'partial tip bearers': these bear fruit buds on spurs as well as the tips of one-year-old shoots. Bramley's Seedling and Worcester Pearmain are two examples of partial tip bearers. Being able to distinguish between the larger fruit buds and the smaller, flatter growth buds is important when identifying spur- and tip-bearing trees.

When maintenance pruning a tree that is over three years old, it is important to follow a few simple rules and not overcomplicate the process. Any dead or diseased growth must be cut out, keeping an eye out for cankers. If cankers are encountered, they need to be removed; the pruning saw should then be cleaned with a suitable sterilant such as methylated spirits before it is used in another part of the tree, to avoid spreading infection. Congested growth in the centre of the tree needs thinning out, as does strong vertical growth. It is worth following the advice that you should be able to throw your hat through the canopy of the tree after you have pruned it. The removal of dead, diseased, damaged and congested growth is the main part of the pruning process; additional work may improve the tree, but getting the basics done first is important.

Winter-Pruning Systems

There are two simple winter-pruning systems for apples apart from the previously mentioned spur pruning. The first involves cutting back the leading shoots by a third of their extension growth and leaving the side shoots unpruned apart from vigorous ones growing towards the centre of the tree. These will develop fruit buds as they mature. In the second method, often called regulated pruning, the leading shoots are left unpruned, but when they have become too long, they are cut out completely in favour of a lower branch growing at a wide angle. Very low branches that have been bent down by the weight of fruit can also be removed in favour of those growing at a more favourable angle.

The regulated method of pruning has a lot of advantages. It is simple and involves relatively few cuts with a pruning saw, rather than having to make numerous cuts with secateurs. A tree can be pruned with no more than a dozen cuts made, and because it is time-saving, it is the method favoured by many commercial growers. In addition, the regulated pruning method prevents the trees from becoming too large and helps to maintain a balance between old and new wood.

When pruning out branches, it is important that the pruning cuts are not made flush with the main stems: the small swelling at the base of the branch – the branch collar – must be left intact to enable rapid healing of the pruning wound. It was once common practice to use a wound paint to seal pruning cuts in the belief that it would hasten healing and prevent infection. These wound paints are seldom necessary and could only be justified to prevent the spread of an existing disease such as apple canker.

It is better to take out whole branches than leave stubs that can regrow, leading to congested growth.

If scion material for grafting is required from the tree being pruned, delay the operation until late winter such as the end of February, to prevent the best propagation material being removed before it is needed.

Pruning neglected trees is not difficult, but the temptation to make up for years without pruning by making savage cuts must be avoided at all costs. A tree's usual reaction to savage pruning is to make very vigorous and congested growth, most of which will be unproductive. The golden rule is to take no more than 20 per cent of the tree's canopy off in a single year, which may mean deferring some pruning work for subsequent years. Allowing the prunings to accumulate in a single pile is a good way to monitor the volume of material being cut out – it is better to under-prune rather than over-prune.

These properly pruned bush apple trees have an open centre with well spaced branches to let light and air into the crown.

Restorative Pruning

The priority when carrying out the restorative pruning of apple trees is to take out diseased and damaged growth, followed by rubbing, crossing or congested growth. Care needs to be taken when removing thicker branches as this will create large open wounds and can be hazardous. If a large limb needs removal, it may be advisable to employ a professional tree surgeon to undertake the work.

If you decide to remove a large branch, it is best to remove it in several stages, as smaller pieces are easier to untangle from the tree and there is less chance of personal injury caused by a falling heavy object. To prevent the risk of bark tearing as the cut branch falls an undercut is made, and then a downward cut, leaving a stub that is subsequently removed.

Once all diseased, damaged, congested and strongly upright growth has been removed and the canopy opened up to allow light and air to penetrate, the tree can be easily managed using the regulated pruning system.

Suckers

Growths arising directly from the rootstock are unwanted and need immediate removal. Suckers arising from the ground need to be cut from their point of origin from the root system, rather than at ground level. It may be possible to detach those suckers with some roots attached and grow these on as rootstocks for grafting.

Savage pruning of mature trees leads to problems and does not increase productivity.

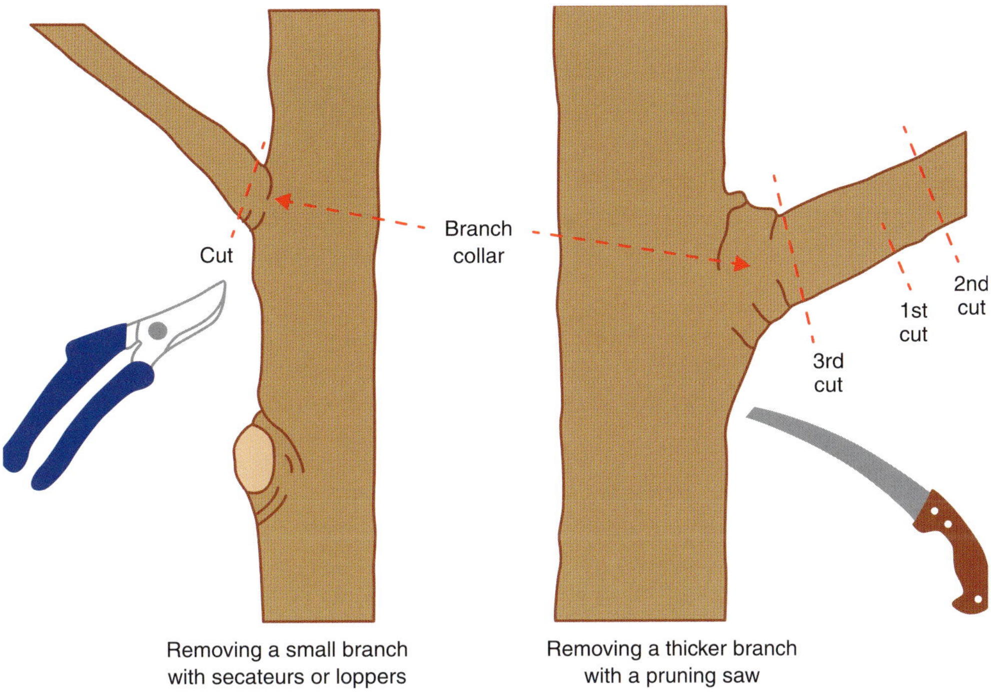

Limb removal in stages.

Suckers are growths that come directly from the rootstock. They need immediate removal.

Growing Cordon, Stepover, Espalier and Fan-Trained Apples

Espalier and cordon fruit trees provide an excellent solution to the common problem of putting many trees in one small area. Cordons are usually grown as single-stemmed trees grown at an angle of about 45 degrees (oblique cordons), and these are trained on to a post-and-wire system. Variants of the oblique single-cordon system include single vertical cordons and double vertical or oblique cordons.

Cordons

Cordons require training on a post-and-wire system that can be placed in front of a sunny wall or fence, or they can be grown in the open to make a decorative and productive screen. An alternative to the post-and-wire system is to train the trees over a strong metal arch. It is possible to use a lot of creativity when training cordon trees to make them outstanding garden features.

When selecting varieties for cordon culture, it is essential to pick those that are spur-bearing and will fruit on short lateral growths. Tip bearers and partial tip bearers are generally unsuitable for cordon culture. Unfortunately, many fruit-tree growers will offer totally unsuitable varieties as cordons, so it is worth checking the suitability of a variety before buying.

It is also worth avoiding very vigorous varieties such as Laxton's Superb for cordon culture, and the trees should be grafted on to a dwarfing rootstock. On fertile soils, M9 is a good choice; on poorer ones, M26 is more suitable. Cordon trees are easy to manage: their restricted size means that harvesting is simple, and no ladders are required. It is possible to grow early, mid-season and late-maturing varieties in one small area and get a succession of fruiting. Pears can also be trained as cordons using the same cultural techniques.

The vigour of cordon trees is kept in check by summer rather than winter pruning. Growing the main stem at an oblique angle rather than vertically will also supress vigour.

In most situations, cordons are planted between 60 and 90cm (24 and 36in) apart. The wider spacings will apply to poorer soils or trees on more vigorous root-stocks. Cordon trees have a similar cost to bush and half-standard trees, and planting a run of cordon trees can incur considerable cost. Grafting your own varieties on to suitable dwarfing rootstocks, or purchasing one-year-old maiden trees can lead to a considerable cost saving.

Vertical Cordons: Minarette, Ballerina and Starline Apples

The simplest cordon growing system is to use vertical cordons. Minarette trees are grown with a single leader and have their laterals hard pruned to produce spur systems for fruiting. Most spur-bearing varieties are suitable for training as Minarette cordons if they are not too vigorous. Minarette apples are harder to keep in shape than Ballerina and Starline varieties, which are naturally columnar.

Ballerina trees originated from a mutation on a tree of the American variety 'McIntosh'. A branch on a tree was seen growing only short laterals. Trees propagated from this branch replicated these characteristics, and these were used in a breeding programme to create new varieties. The appeal of Ballerina trees was that they took up little space and required minimal pruning. Unfortunately, Ballerina trees share the same disadvantages of their McIntosh parent, namely disease susceptibility and fruit with a moderate flavour. Starline apples have similar

Belgian lattice is a very attractive way of growing apples, as well as being productive.

growth characteristics to Ballerina trees but have better-tasting apples and better disease resistance.

Cordons are best trained on a structure consisting of three horizontal wires spaced 60cm (24in) apart. The lowest wire should be 30cm (12in) from the ground. If the wires are attached to a fence post or wall they should be spaced at least 10cm (4in) from the structure using strong eyelets. Strong, fencing-grade wire must be used, and it should be tensioned using wire tensioners. If the post-and-wire support is free-standing, the end posts should be strutted. The posts should be strong enough to support the cordons: 2.4m (8ft) fence posts 7.5cm (3in) wide are ideal. The posts should be pressure-treated against decay. The posts should be buried to a depth of 60cm (24in) allowing 1.8m (6ft) above ground.

Oblique cordons are planted at an angle of 45 degrees and are tied to a bamboo cane using a soft tie. The leading shoot is left unpruned, and any lateral shoots are pruned back to three buds. Thereafter, only summer pruning is used to regulate growth. For southern parts of the UK summer pruning is usually carried out in August when the annual growth has ceased. In the north and wetter parts of the country, this is usually delayed until September, when a large terminal bud forms on side shoots, indicating the cessation of annual growth. Side shoots longer than 22cm (9in) are shortened back to three buds, and growths shorter than 22cm (the length of a pair of secateurs) are shortened back to a single leaf beyond the basal cluster from which the growth originated. The leading shoots are usually left unpruned. Once the leading shoot has reached the top of the cane, it is treated in the same way as lateral shoots.

The length of an oblique cordon and therefore its cropping capacity can be increased by reducing its angle with the ground from 45 degrees to no less than 35 degrees. This is an operation that involves some risk of breaking the tree and ruining it. My advice is not to bother.

There are a few instances when winter pruning of oblique cordons can be justified. If few laterals develop from the leading shoots, new growth from the leader can be reduced by a third to encourage branching. Dormant buds can be encouraged to grow laterally by using the technique of notching. A small, crescent-shaped nick is cut into the bark above the bud, and this will reduce the dominance of the uppermost bud. If spurs become congested and produce masses of small, low-quality fruits, cutting back the spurs to 5cm (2in) off the main stem to encourage new growth can be worthwhile.

Ballerina and Starline apple trees require very little, if any, pruning. Minarette and other vertical cordon trees are pruned the same way as oblique cordons, except that the annual growth on the leading shoots is cut by a third each winter.

Multiple-stemmed cordon apples are a very intensive form of fruit cultivation.

Double, triple or even quadruple vertical cordons can make excellent specimens for growing in large pots. Just a word of caution: well-trained specimens can be mouth-wateringly expensive!

Stepover Trees

Stepover trees are comparatively easy to train from maiden trees. The support system is made using stakes of about 75cm (30in) in length and spaced approximately 1.5 to 2m (5 to 6ft) apart. Strong wire is attached to these posts about 45cm (18in) above ground and tensioned. Ready-formed stepover trees have two horizontal branches extending in different directions from the trunk, and can be positioned for best effect allowing for extension growth of the main horizontal branches. If training from a maiden tree, select an 'unfeathered' one with no side branches if possible. The tree is planted vertically next to a post, and other stepover trees can be planted next to other posts, so they are spaced between 1.5 to 2m (5 to 6ft) apart.

Over the course of the growing season, the leading shoot is gradually tied down to the horizontal wire. This operation must be carried out incrementally, and it is a good idea to tie the leader in several places with soft string or cord. Side growths arising from the leader should be pruned to three leaves. The leading shoot is left unpruned until it has reached its required length, and it is then pruned to just above a bud. Subsequent pruning is carried out in late summer in the same manner as described for cordon apples. As with cordon apples, old and unproductive spurs can be shortened back to make new fruiting wood.

An alternative to bending the leading shoot is to prune the leader very hard to about 30cm (12in) above ground, and select two buds either side of the leader to develop into the left- and right-side branches. The resultant growths from these buds should be trained along canes at an angle of 45 degrees. At the end of the growing season, the two structural branches should be carefully tied down to the horizontal wire.

Espalier Trees

Espalier trees provide another solution to the problem of growing fruit trees where space is limited; they can also be very decorative. Fruit is borne on short spurs on long horizontal branches, and like cordons, this method of training is suitable only for spur-fruiting varieties rather than tip bearers. Like cordons, summer pruning is carried out to restrict vigour; the work is carried out in August or September, with laterals being shortened to one or three buds depending upon their length.

Espalier trees can be trained with one to four horizontal tiers. A four-tier espalier will need to be trained on to a large wall or framework. A single-tiered tree is usually called a stepover or horizontal cordon, and can make a decorative and productive edging to a path or garden divider.

Espaliers can be purchased as a ready-trained stepover, two- or three-tiered trees with a price reflecting their age and the amount of training undertaken in the nursery. They are also difficult to transport, and many nurseries insist on collection by the customer. Stepover trees are often grafted on to a very dwarfing rootstock such as M27. Two-tiered espaliers are usually grafted on to the semi-dwarfing MM106 rootstock, and three- and four-tiered trees on to the semi-vigorous MM111. It is not difficult to train your own espalier tree from an inexpensive maiden tree, or cheaper still, to propagate your own tree.

Espaliers, like cordon trees, need a strong support framework. If grown directly against a wall or fence, the support wires should be kept at least 10cm (4in) from the fence using eyelets. If using a fence for support, it is always a good idea to check it is sound, and to replace any rotting posts before fixing support wires. Strong wires are needed, and these should be tensioned using fence tensioners. If the support system is freestanding, the end posts should be strutted to allow the wires to be properly tensioned.

If buying already trained espaliers, it is a good idea to measure the height of the lateral branches before fixing the support wires to the posts, to ensure a good fit. If several trees are bought and there is variance in the heights of the branches, this should not be a major concern as the branches should be sufficiently pliable to enable adjustment.

If training espaliers from scratch, the horizontal wires should be spaced about 45cm (18in) apart. The height of the posts will depend on the number of tiers required.

Espalier trees should be planted between 4.5 and 6m (15 and 20ft) apart. The exact spacing will be governed by the natural vigour of the apple variety, the rootstock, and the soil fertility.

When training a maiden tree into an espalier, the tree is best planted in winter and the leading shoot pruned back to about 30cm (12in). This savage pruning will stimulate growth buds in spring, when three shoots are selected: one shoot will form the central leader, and the other two will form the first set of tiers. The central leader is grown up a vertical cane, and the two lateral branches are trained at an angle of 45 degrees. Growing at 45 degrees rather than horizontally will impart a little more vigour to the laterals. At the end of the growing season, the lateral branches are tied down to the horizontal wire and the central leader is pruned 30cm (12in) above the first support wire. The lateral branches are left unpruned.

The next stage is the same as creating the first tier. Three buds are selected, one to create a central leader (if another tier is required), and two shoots are grown at 45 degrees to make the second tier. The shoots forming the second tier are tied to the horizontal support wire at the end of the growing season. The formative pruning process continues until there is the required number of tiers. Once this has happened, any extension growth from the central leader is pruned in summer as a fruiting spur.

Fan-Trained Trees

Fan-trained trees provide an alternative to espaliers and cordons for wall culture. A fan tree consists of a short trunk from which framework shoots radiate at approximately equal angles. Ornamental in their own right, fan-trained trees can take advantage of the microclimate of a sunny wall or fence. As with espaliers and cordons, a spur-fruiting variety should be selected for fan culture. The choice of rootstock should be matched to the space available: trees on the semi-dwarfing M26 rootstock can accommodate a wall space of 2m (6.5ft) high and 3m (10ft) wide, on MM106 the width can be increased to 4m (13ft), and on the more vigorous M111 rootstock the allocated width can be 5m (16ft).

The rootstock is not the only factor that determines the vigour of the tree: a naturally vigorous variety such as Laxton's Superb will make a larger tree on the same rootstock as a compact variety such as Sunset. Soil fertility will also influence vigour. Fan-trained trees can be bought with a lot of the framework already in place, but this is an expensive option. In addition, the availability of trained trees is much smaller than bush trees, so it may not be possible to buy the variety that you want on the rootstock of your choice. The purchase of maiden trees, or grafting your own, may add a couple of years' wait until the trees become productive, but at a considerable cost saving.

As with all trained fruit, a strong post-and-wire support may be necessary. On long runs, the end posts should be braced, and the wires tensioned. If the fence post or wall is used as the support, the wires must be kept at least 5cm (2in) from it using eyelets. The bottom horizontal wire should be positioned about 45cm (18in) above ground level, followed by other wires spaced 15cm (6in) apart. The wires should be kept at least 5cm (2in) from the wall.

Starting with a maiden tree that has made a season's growth after grafting, the leading shoot is cut back hard to about 45cm (18in) above ground, leaving three strong buds. The growth from two of these buds will be used to create two framework shoots, while the third bud is retained as an insurance.

Two canes are placed at a 45-degree angle on either side of the main trunk, and two shoots are trained up these canes, with all other growth removed from the main trunk. The following spring, the two framework branches are reduced by two-thirds to an upward-facing bud. When the tree comes back into growth, four shoots are selected to extend the framework. Two evenly spaced shoots are selected on the upper side of each branch: one is selected at about the mid-point on the lower side of the branch, and one at the end to extend the branch. The cuts should be made to an upward-facing bud. These shoots are tied in at 30 degrees to the main arm, ideally to short bamboo canes attached to the training wires. Subsequent training involves a little improvisation, as extension growth from the main shoots is tied in where space permits. All growth growing towards the wall or fence must be cut out, and shoots growing outwards pruned to one leaf.

Once the framework of a fan has been achieved, pruning is mainly summer pruning to restrict vigour and encourage fruit bud production. The technique is the same as for other trained fruit, with shoots longer than 20cm (8in) being shortened to three leaves above the basal cluster and regrowth after pruning to one leaf. Growths emerging from the spurs should be shortened to one leaf. Summer pruning is carried out in July or August for areas where extension growth is late to ripen. Overgrown spurs can be reduced in winter as the fans mature.

Watering and Feeding

Established apple trees should not require additional watering in most seasons. The only possible exception to this rule concerns apples prone to bitter pit that are growing in a sandy soil. Dry soil can prevent the uptake of calcium from the soil and lead to this disorder. Newly planted trees may need additional watering during dry periods in summer until their roots become established. The golden rule with watering young plants is to water thoroughly and relatively infrequently. A daily sprinkling of water encourages surface rooting, rather than deep rooting, which makes the tree more resilient to drought. A watering can is more useful than a hose, and the water should be applied gently so that it soaks in gradually rather than running off the surface. Specially made bags that hold water and release it slowly over a period of time can be useful for the establishment of young trees.

Mulching helps to retain soil moisture as well as supressing the growth of annual weeds. A variety of organic materials can be used, such as composted bark and home-made compost. Mulch should be applied to moist, weed-free soil to a depth of about 5cm (2in). The mulch must not be in contact with the stem of the tree to prevent fungal infection.

Although many trees growing in a fertile soil will crop reasonably well without the addition of fertiliser, a moderate application in spring may help to increase growth, leading to better yields. Different fertilisers

Tree watering bags are useful for newly planted trees to overcome water stress whilst they are becoming established.

have different application rates depending on their concentration of nutrients. Feeding and mulching can be combined if the mulch material contains nutrients such as comfrey foliage and well-rotted farmyard manure. Cooking apples favour a balanced mix of nitrogen, phosphorus and potassium, while dessert apples favour a higher concentration of potassium.

Fruit Thinning

The removal of excess fruit – or thinning – is useful for a variety of reasons. Keeping too many fruits results in small fruits and places an excessive strain on the tree. A heavily fruiting branch is liable to break, and this will create an opening for fungal diseases and reduce future cropping capacity. After producing a heavy crop one year, the tree is liable to take a sabbatical year in terms of fruiting and yield a moderate crop. This can lead to 'biennial bearing', which is a common feature for many apples such as Laxton's Superb and Blenheim Orange.

Fruit thinning should be carried out after the 'June drop'. Trees will naturally abort excess and poorly pollinated fruits to avoid excessive strain being placed on the tree. Attacks by apple sawfly will also result in the loss of young fruits in June. Therefore, moderate feeding by sawflies can actually be beneficial and assist with the fruit-thinning process. As the young fruits develop from July onwards, very small, misshapen and damaged fruits can be removed using a small-bladed pair of secateurs. In clusters of fruitlets, the large and misshapen 'king fruit' should be removed to give the others room to develop. Fruits on the underside of branches that will not receive enough light to ripen and develop sweetness should be sacrificed in favour of those receiving more light. Cooking apples should be thinned more than dessert apples. Cooking apples should be thinned to achieve a spacing of approximately 15 to 25cm (6 to 10in) between fruits, and dessert apples reduced to one or two fruits every 10 to 15cm (4 to 6in) of branch.

Harvesting and Storage

Apples are harvested when fully ripe, when the fruit can be detached from the tree using a 90-degree twist; this readiness to harvest is usually seen by fruit starting to drop from the tree. Early apples such as Beauty of Bath and Irish Peach need to be picked and eaten almost immediately as their quality diminishes rapidly once picked. Early apples are best grown as small trees or cordons as it is very difficult to use up the crop before it deteriorates. Mid- and late-season apples need a period of storage before the fruits achieve their optimum sweetness. The general rule is the later cropping the variety, the longer the period of storage. Cooking apples can be picked and stored as soon as the fruits start to fall from the tree, and most eaters are picked when slightly underripe. Some varieties such as Golden Delicious and Jonagold are best left on the tree to obtain maximum ripeness to achieve a pleasant, sweet flavour. Dual-purpose varieties such as Charles Ross and James Grieve may have an early picking for fruits used for cooking, and a later one for fruits to be eaten fresh.

Harvesting apples needs to be done safely. If a ladder is needed, an orchard tripod ladder is a much safer option than an ordinary domestic one, and is usually easier to manoeuvre between branches. A fruit-picking bag is a useful accessory, particularly if picking from a ladder. Fruit harvesting tools are available from a variety of suppliers. The tool detaches the fruit from the branch, allowing it to fall into a small cloth bag. This means that the fruit can be picked from on the ground, but manoeuvring the tool and harvesting the fruit can be a time-consuming and sometimes frustrating process.

One hazard of fruit picking is the attention of wasps, which will feed on fruits already damaged by bird pecking. Wasps become a nuisance in late summer when the queens stop laying eggs. The worker wasps collect insects during the summer to feed to the larvae, which then feed the adults with a sweet nutritious substance. Adults are incapable of digesting insects and rely on the food from the larvae in summer. As autumn approaches, the adults are denied their

Apple storage cabinets provide optimal conditions for storing apples. They can be bought ready-made or can be a DIY project.

usual food and turn to fruit and other sugary substances for sustenance. But fruits soon ferment, and the wasps feeding on them become intoxicated and this creates aggressive behaviour. A wasp sting can attract the attention of other wasps when close to their nest, and this could lead to multiple stings with possible serious consequences for people who suffer an allergic reaction.

Being aware of the presence of wasp nests is a good way of preventing stings, although about 70 per cent of nests occur underground. Apparently wearing white or pale-coloured clothing helps to minimise wasp attacks, though this is something that I have not yet put to the test!

Apples can be stored in flat trays in a cool but frost-free location such as a well-insulated shed or garage. Fruit must be kept away from strong-smelling substances such as solvents and other chemicals. Mice can be an absolute menace, and have the annoying habit of taking small bites out of every stored apple rather than devouring a single one. Cardboard fruit trays and their inserts may be available free from greengrocers or supermarkets.

For the keen fruit grower, a purpose-built storage rack with slatted shelves is ideal but a rather expensive option. However they are stored, apples need to be inspected regularly and any fruit showing decay removed immediately.

For short-term storage, apples can be kept in polythene bags folded at the top and placed in the refrigerator for several weeks. Early cookers may be cooked into purée and frozen.

CHAPTER 4

GROWING PEARS

Botanically, pears are a close cousin of the apple, both belonging to the rose family Rosaceae. Like apples, pears originate in East Asia and the move westwards was facilitated by man and other mammals. Pears developed around two geographical areas, China and Asia Minor, with the evolution of the spherical 'Asian pears' and the pyriform European pears. The evolution of cultivated pears is as complex as that of apples and involves numerous species.

Pear production is eclipsed by apple production, with the worldwide production of apples being over three times that of pears by weight. China remains the main producer of pears, but production is spread across the globe, occurring in all continents except Antarctica.

It is estimated that there are about 3,000 varieties of pear in cultivation, with the most popular variety being Williams Bon Chretien (incorrectly called Bartlett in North America and Australia). The cultivation of pears can be traced back to 2000BCE in China, and they were popular with the Romans for eating fresh or stewing with honey. Pears were also fermented into an alcoholic beverage that would later become known as perry.

The Normans with their enthusiasm for orchard fruits brought pears to Britain, and references were made in English medieval literature to recipes that included the fruit. The pears of this period were likely to be hard and required a long period of cooking before they were soft enough to eat. In this respect, these pears resembled their very close botanical cousin, the quince. Henry VIII had a keen interest in fruit production, and under his reign, more varieties of pear were brought to England via the continent to be grown in his Kent orchards.

Queen Elizabeth I of England commented on the beauty of the black pear (a dark-skinned cooking variety that is not black) during a visit to Worcester. So impressed was she with the fruit, Elizabeth ordered that it should feature on the coat of arms of the city, which it still does today.

During the Stuart era, the acreage of pears in England increased greatly, with the cultivation of perry pears in response to concerns about the availability of wine from Europe. The interest in pear cultivation in Georgian and Victorian Britain followed a path similar to that for apples, with the Victorian enthusiasm for horticulture resulting in new varieties that remain popular today. The contribution made by French and Belgian horticulturists in developing new varieties of pear must be acknowledged – this is evident by the number of popular varieties with French names.

In Britain, the cultivation of pears is less popular than apples. This is partly because most pear varieties require a warm autumn in order for the fruit to ripen properly, making the crop less reliable than apples.

Many pear varieties lack the storage properties of apples, and this was highlighted by the comment made by the American essayist Ralph Waldo Emerson, who said: 'There are only ten minutes in the life of a pear when it is perfect to eat.' That is rather extreme, but it is very frustrating to have a bowl of ripe pears turn rotten within a few days. The expression 'as rotten as a pear' is not without basis. It is possible to select pear varieties that have a comparatively long shelf life, such as Winter Nelis, or the Asian pears that can be kept for up to two months. Storage life is an important consideration when deciding which varieties to grow.

The cultivation of pears by amateur gardeners has been made easier by the introduction of dwarfing rootstocks and new varieties. In previous decades, pears would be grafted on to pear seedling rootstocks, resulting in very large trees that took a long time to come into bearing and were difficult to manage. The saying 'you plant pears for your heirs' acknowledged this drawback. The use of quince (a very close relative of the pear) as a rootstock started in the Angers region of France. Pears grafted on to quince made smaller trees than those grafted on to seedling pear, and were more precocious. Most pear trees are now grafted on to quince rootstocks because of these advantages.

Pears fare best in a sheltered, sunny position, and are particularly suited to growing against south- or west-facing walls as fans, espaliers or cordons.

Pear Beurre Hardy – a large pear with an exquisite flavour.

Pear Concorde – combining the attributes of its parents, Conference and Doyenne du Comice, this variety is a good combination of reliability and flavour.

Selected Varieties

European pears are considered to have a superior flavour, but Asian varieties have a pleasing crispness and can be stored for weeks in a fridge. The rounded fruits of Asian pears resemble apples in shape, and the trees are particularly attractive, with bronze young growths and vivid autumnal tints. Asian pears (also known as 'nashi' or 'Chinese pears') do not grow well on the dwarfing quince rootstocks used by European pears, and are usually grafted on to more vigorous pear rootstocks; as a result they will make larger trees. They appreciate plenty of sunshine to ripen the fruit. They are best suited to the south of England, rather than the north.

Conference – a deservedly popular pear with sweet, melting flesh. Unusually it can set fruit without pollination.

Pear Improved Fertility – sweet juicy fruits and disease resistance are some of the attributes of this variety. It is also self-fertile.

Pear Invincible – a useful pear variety for difficult situations where other varieties might fail.

Pear Doyenne du Comice – considered to be the best flavoured pear of all, this variety needs a warm summer to be at its best.

Asian pear Kumoi – considered to be the best-flavoured Asian pear of all.

Asian Pear Shinseiki – a very reliable cropper, and it makes a most attractive garden tree.

Pear Onward – a deservedly popular variety, and very suitable for garden culture. It will not pollinate Doyenne du Comice, and vice versa.

Pear Williams – the world's most popular pear variety. It is grown in the USA and Australia as Bartlett.

Benita (Hybrid Pear)

Benita is a cross between a European pear (Pyrus communis) and an Asian pear (Pyrus pyrifolia), and combines the attributes of both parents. It has the superior flavour of the European pear with the crispness and storage properties of its Asian counterpart. It has good disease resistance. It is picked in September and can store until December. Pollination group 2.

Beth (European Pear)

Beth is a small pear with little commercial appeal, but it is a good choice for the amateur grower. The attractive fruits are pale yellow with a pink flush. The juicy flesh has a melting texture. The compact habit of the tree makes it a good choice where space is restricted. It is harvested in September and needs eating soon afterwards. Pollination group 3.

Beurre Hardy (European Pear)

Beurre Hardy is a French variety that is deservedly popular in the UK; it is also a personal favourite. The skin is russeted and rough, but the flesh is soft and juicy with a pleasing rosewater flavour. The fruits tend to be large, and cropping is good and reliable. The tree makes strong, upright growth, and the spring blossom and autumn foliage are particularly pleasing. Pollination group 4.

Beurre Superfin (European Pear)

Grown for its outstanding flavour, Beurre Superfin is best grown on a warm, sheltered site. The fruits turn pale yellow when ripe. Pollination group 3.

Black Worcester (European pear)

Black Worcester is the pear that features in the coat of arms for the city of Worcester. The distinctive fruits are dark green and covered by a brown russet, and often develop a purplish flush. The cropping is heavy and reliable for this cooking pear. The fruit, picked in October, can store until February. Pollination group 4.

Catalliac (European Pear)

Catalliac rivals Black Worcester as the best cooking pear. The green-yellow fruits develop a red flush. It has vigorous growth and crops heavily. The fruit, picked in October, can store until February. Pollination group 4.

Concorde (European Pear)

The variety Concorde has so much to commend it. It was made by crossing Conference with Doyenne du Comice, and has managed to combine the best attributes of both parents – namely the reliability of Conference and the excellent flavour of Doyenne du Comice. To add to its appeal, it is self-fertile and disease-resistant. The fruit is harvested in September and may last until November. Pollination group 4.

Conference (European Pear)

Named in honour of the British National Conference in 1885, this variety has retained its popularity with amateur and professional growers, and is the most commonly grown pear in the UK. The yellowish green fruits have a brown russet and are sweet and juicy. Fruits can sometimes set without pollination, and these are much thinner than pollinated fruits. The variety is self-fertile and trouble-free. There is a variant available called Moors Giant, which was discovered in Belgium. The fruits can be up to 40 per cent larger than the regular variety. Pollination group 3.

Doyenne du Comice (European Pear)

Considered one of the finest flavoured pears, Doyenne du Comice needs pampering with a warm, sheltered location; it is a good choice for wall culture on a south- or west-facing wall. Like many excellent varieties, this one originates from the Angers region of France. The yellow fruits can have a red flush and have a rich, juicy flavour. The variety is rather prone to scab. The fruits can be harvested in October and may be kept until November. This variety will not pollinate Onward, and vice versa. Pollination group 4.

Gorham (European Pear)

Gorham is a hybrid of Williams and is considered to have a superior flavour. The pale yellow fruits have a sweet, musky flavour. It is self-fertile and a good pollinator for other varieties. Picked in September, it will last until October. Pollination group 4.

Improved Fertility (European Pear)

The sweet, juicy fruits of Improved Fertility are small to medium-sized and can be used for both eating fresh and cooking. It is a reliable cropper that is self-fertile and disease-resistant. Harvest in late September and store until mid-October. Pollination group 3.

Invincible (European Pear)

Invincible is a very hardy variety that can flower a second time if the first blossoms are damaged by frost. It may not score top marks for flavour, but it is reasonable. The fruit is suitable for cooking as well as eating fresh. Its main attribute is its reliability in far from ideal situations, and it crops heavily and from an early age. It is a good choice for an exposed site and may succeed where other varieties fail. It can be harvested in September and will keep to November. Pollination group 2.

Kumoi (Asian Pear)

The attractive round fruits of the variety Kumoi are covered in a light brown russet and have a sweet, mild flavour with a hint of strawberry. This is considered the best-flavoured Asian pear. The fruits are picked in September when fully ripe and will store for several weeks in a fridge. It is partially self-fertile, but fruit set can be improved using another Asian pear or a European one as a pollinator. Pollination group 3.

Louise Bonne of Jersey (European Pear)

This variety produces small, pale yellow fruits with a red flush; they have juicy, melting flesh with a sweet flavour. A dependable variety with blossoms showing some frost resistance. Harvest the fruits in September, and they will keep for a few weeks. It is unsuitable as a pollinator for Williams, and vice versa. Pollination group 2.

Merton Pride (European Pear)

Merton Pride is a triploid variety so will need a self-fertile pollinator, or the pollinating variety will need its own pollinator. The large, pale yellow fruits have some russet. The fruit is exceptionally juicy and has a good flavour, but it is not a good keeper. Cropping can be moderate. Harvest in September. Pollination group 3.

Moonglow (European Pear)

Moonglow is an American variety that produces large, yellow-skinned fruits that are sweet, soft and juicy. It can be picked in August and kept until September. Pollination group 3.

Obelisk (European Pear)

Obelisk is a new variety hailing from Slovakia that offers the amateur gardener three useful advantages: its naturally compact habit means that it is useful for confined spaces; it has good storage properties; and it is self-fertile. The small green fruits often have a red flush, and have firm, moderately flavoured flesh. The fruits are picked in October and can store until January. Pollination group 3.

Onward (European Pear)

Onward is a variety raised in Britain; it produces juicy, medium-sized fruit with excellent flavour. It is a reliable cropper and an excellent choice for garden cultivation. Although it is in the same pollination group as Doyenne du Comice, it is ineffective as a pollinator for this variety, and vice versa. Harvested in September, it will keep for a few weeks. Pollination group 4.

Packham's Triumph (European Pear)

Packham's Triumph is an Australian variety that is popular with commercial growers in that country. Its compact growth makes it a good choice where space is limited, and it has good keeping qualities. The pale yellow fruits sometimes have a brown russet. The fruits are sometimes covered in small bumps, but these do not affect their eating or storage qualities. The juicy flesh has a fine, musky flavour. Picked in October, the fruits can keep until December. Pollination group 3.

Pitmaston Duchess (European Pear)

Pitmaston Duchess is an unusual variety that is partially self-fertile despite being a triploid. The flavour of the golden-yellow fruit is exceptional, but cropping is moderate. Growth is vigorous, so it needs to be grafted on to a dwarfing rootstock if space is an issue. Like all triploids, choose two pollination partners or a self-fertile single one. Picked in September, the variety will store for a few weeks. Pollination group 4.

Shinseiki (Asian pear)

Shinseiki is a large-fruited Asian pear with pale yellow fruits that have firm, sweet flesh. The cropping is reliable. The tree is particularly ornamental, with bronze young growths, attractive white flowers and autumn tints. Pollination group 3.

Williams' Bon Chrétien (European Pear)

Williams' Bon Chrétien is the world's most commonly cultivated pear. In North America and Australia it is known as Bartlett after the American nurseryman who imported it from England. It is popular for canning, and if you have eaten tinned pears, it is highly likely that you have eaten this variety. The pear was found as a chance seedling in Aldermaston in Berkshire in the garden of Mr Wheeler, a schoolmaster. The garden passed to another schoolmaster, Mr Stair, who allowed Mr Williams, a nurseryman from Turnham Green in London, to propagate the variety. The sweet, musky flavour of the yellow fruit is refreshing. The growth is compact, but the foliage is rather prone to scab. It is one of the best pears for growing in the north of England, and is a possibility for growing on a north-facing wall. The variety Sensation is a red-skinned variant of Williams. The fruit is picked in late August and is best eaten soon afterwards. This variety is unsuitable as a pollinator for Louise Bonne of Jersey and vice versa. Pollination group 3.

Winter Nelis (European Pear)

Winter Nelis is a very late pear and useful for extending the season. The small pears are covered in russet and have a sweet, delicious flavour. It is a good variety for growing in the north of England. The fruit is picked in November and will store until January. Pollination group 4.

Rootstocks

The use of quince as a dwarfing rootstock has made pear growing much easier. Pear varieties grafted on to seedling pears produced large trees that were slow to come into bearing and difficult to manage. The main rootstock for pears is Quince A, and it will produce a tree between 3 and 6m (10 and 20ft) in height. Quince C is less common and produces slightly smaller trees, between 3 and 5m (10 and 16ft) in height. Trees tend to come into bearing sooner with this rootstock than Quince A. Quince C is a less dependable rootstock and is less commonly used by nurseries. A recent development is the Quince 'Eline' rootstock that has a very dwarfing effect, and the trees tend to have a narrower habit. An additional effect of the Eline rootstock is that fruit russeting is reduced. Trees on this rootstock can be kept at about 2m (7ft) in height; it therefore provides an easy way to grow several pear varieties in a limited space.

Some varieties of pear demonstrate an incompatibility with Quince rootstocks, notably Williams' Bon Chrétien, in which the graft may start to fail after several years. The problem is resolved using an 'interstock', when a quince-compatible variety such as Doyenne du Comice is grafted on to the Quince rootstock and the Williams' Bon Chrétien is grafted on to this. There is a variant of Williams' Bon Chrétien that is graft compatible with quince rootstocks – my initial trials of this variety appear favourable.

Asian pears do not favour quince rootstocks and need to be grafted on to a pear species. The semi-vigorous Pyrodwarf rootstock produces a tree intermediate in size between a dwarf tree on a quince rootstock and one grafted on to seedling pear. As well as the Pyrodwarf rootstock, Asian pears are grafted on to a Chinese (non-edible) pear species, *Pyrus betulifolia*. Asian pears grafted on to these rootstocks can grow between 6 and 8m (20 and 26ft) in height.

Where there is incompatibility between a pear variety and a rootstock, an intermediate variety is used between the rootstock and the desired variety. This is known as a pear interstock.

Pollination

Like apples, some pear varieties are self-fertile, others are partially self-fertile, and the majority require pollination from a different variety of pear. European and Asian pears can cross-pollinate but apples and pears cannot. There are a few instances of incompatibility between pear varieties for pollination. For example, Williams' Bon Chrétien and Louise Bonne of Jersey will not cross-pollinate, and nor will Doyenne du Comice and Onward. Some varieties of pear are triploid, such as Merton Pride, and these cannot be used as pollinators on account of their sterile pollen. The variety Conference can set fruit without pollination; the unpollinated fruits are abnormally thin but are just as delicious as pollinated ones.

The pollination of self-fertile pear varieties can be improved by having a pollination partner of a different variety.

Most pear varieties fall within three pollination groups: groups 2, 3 and 4. As with apples, varieties in the same or adjacent groups can cross-pollinate.

Pears tend to flower slightly earlier than apples so there is a greater risk of frost damage to the blossoms. The variety Invincible can produce a second flush of blossom if the first is frost-damaged, and the flowers of Winter Nelis have good frost resistance. Trained fruit can be protected from frost with horticultural fleece.

Diseases, Disorders and Pests

Pears have fewer problems with pests and diseases than apples. However, this does not mean they can be considered trouble-free. Careful monitoring of the trees and timely action to minimise attacks is essential to keep pests and diseases at bay.

Diseases

Pear Rust

Pear rust is a fungal disease that has become increasingly common and is now widespread. In common with many rust diseases, it has an alternative host of junipers, and the fungus overwinters on these conifers. The symptoms of pear rust are very distinctive, with bright orange spots with brown patches on the corresponding undersides that produce gall-like outgrowths. These outgrowths contain the fruiting bodies of the fungus and release wind-borne spores that are unable to infect pear but infect the alternative host, juniper, instead. The infected junipers produce outgrowths in spring that can only infect pears. In continental Europe, the fungus can overwinter on pears in bark cankers, but this is very rare in the UK.

Pear rust is a common but not serious fungal disease of pears. The fungus overwinters on juniper.

Like many rust diseases, pear rust is difficult to control. Currently there are no permitted fungicides for the control of rust on edible pears, though there are some products that can be used on purely ornamental varieties. Pulling off affected leaves is unlikely to offer any form of control as the fruiting bodies on the undersides of the foliage produce spores that can only infect junipers. In addition, foliage removal is likely to weaken the tree. The removal of junipers in the vicinity has limited value as the spores released in spring are highly mobile and can travel several kilometres on wind currents.

Pear Scab

Pear scab is very similar to apple scab in terms of symptoms, the effect on cropping, and control measures. It is caused by the fungus *Venturia pyrina* whereas apple scab is caused by *Venturia inaequalis*. Pear scab cannot infect apples, and vice versa. The disease can infect leaves, stems and fruit, and the effect on cropping can be serious. On the foliage, dark green patches turning brown appear on the leaves, which then fall prematurely. Blisters can appear on infected stems and these blisters can provide entry points for fungal canker. Scabby blotches appear on infected fruit, and more severe infection can result in distortion and cracking of the skin. Minor skin infections will not affect the eating quality of the fruit, but will make it unsaleable for commercial growers.

Whereas commercial growers can use a range of professional fungicides for scab control, these chemicals are unavailable to the amateur grower, who must use cultural methods to reduce infection. The most effective method of minimising pear scab is to select resistant varieties. The potential damage caused by scab warrants disease resistance being a major consideration when selecting varieties. The varieties Doyenne Du Comice and Williams' Bon Chrétien are both prone to scab, whereas Beurre Hardy, Gorham, Catillac, Conference, Concorde, Improved Fertility and Black Worcester are resistant.

The fungus overwinters on fallen leaves and in blisters to reinfect new growth in the spring. Cutting out infected growth during winter pruning, and the removal and disposal of fallen foliage, will help to minimise the spread of this disease.

Canker

Like apples, pears can be affected by canker caused by the fungus *Neonetria ditissima*. The identification and control of this disease has been discussed in Chapter 3: Growing Apples.

Fireblight

Most pathogens of fruit plants are fungal; however, fireblight is a potentially devastating bacterial disease caused by the bacterium Erwinia amylovora. Originating from North America where it is extremely serious, the bacterium gained entry to the UK in 1957. The disease gets its name from the appearance of infected shoots with brown, withered foliage that looks as if it has been scorched by fire. Like many bacterial diseases, its spread is favoured by warm weather, and this explains why it is more prevalent in the United States than Great Britain. The disease affects pears and to a lesser extent, apples. Ornamental and amenity species of trees and shrubs in the rose family Rosaceae – which includes Crataegus (hawthorn), Cotoneaster, Pyracantha and Sorbus – are prone to fireblight infection.

The symptoms of fireblight include withering blossoms, a slimy liquid exuding from infected areas, and the rapid dieback of shoots. The outer wood becomes stained dark brown, and the growing points start to bend downwards, resembling a shepherd's crook. At the junction of infected shoots and main stems, areas of sunken bark (cankers) may form. The cambium also becomes stained with a reddish-brown coloration.

If uncontrolled, this disease can kill the entire tree and rapidly infect whole orchards. When it first arrived in the UK, any infections had to be reported to the then Ministry of Agriculture, Fisheries and Food (MAFF). However, as this disease is now widespread, reporting is only necessary in regions where it has not established a presence, such as the Channel Islands and the Isle of Man.

The disease overwinters in bark cankers, and with the onset of warm, wet and windy weather the bacterial slime oozes out and becomes mobile by the action of wind-blown rain and pollinating insects. The disease infects the inner bark, usually via the blossoms. Fruit trees are mostly in flower in early spring, and the low temperatures help to minimise infections, but some trees may produce a second flush of blossom in summer and that renders them much more susceptible. The pear variety 'Laxton's Superb' (not to be confused with the apple of the same name) tends to produce summer blossom, and this means that it is no longer grown as it poses a risk of fireblight infection. Although a potentially serious disease, fireblight is not as problematic in Britain as it is in other parts of the world; however, climate change may mean that it could become a major problem. In the United States, pear and apple rootstocks are often selected according to their fireblight resistance.

Summer-flowering shrubs such as Pyracantha and Cotoneaster are more prone to fireblight than fruit trees. The Saphyr range of Pyracantha cultivars are credited with good fireblight resistance. Hawthorn is also susceptible, and for this reason, hedges of this plant are not grown around commercial orchards; instead, plants such as alder (Alnus) are used for wind protection. In gardens, hawthorn is a valuable plant for wildlife including pollinators and birds, and its removal as a preventive measure may be hard to justify.

The best control for fireblight is the pruning out of infected wood using sterilised tools. The extent of the infection can be assessed by looking at the areas of stained bark and the cambium below the bark. On small shoots, the pruning cut should be made at least 30cm (12in) beyond the area of infection, and for large branches it should be at least 60cm (24in) beyond infected tissue. Tools must be sterilised using a horticultural sterilant or methylated spirits between cuts. The infected material must be burned immediately. In the case of severe infection, it is advisable to destroy the tree and burn the wood.

There is no chemical control available for fireblight. In the United States, commercial growers have used antibiotics such as Streptomycin to control fireblight, but this is not permissible in the UK due to increasing antibiotic resistance. Different pear varieties have varying levels of fireblight resistance, with Williams' Bon Chrétien and Clapp's Favourite considered susceptible, and Moonglow resistant to the disease.

Pear Stony-Pit Virus

There are several confirmed and suspected virus diseases of pear. Although rare, pear stony-pit virus may be encountered occasionally. Typically the fruit is misshapen and the flesh is gritty and hard, making it almost impossible to cut with a knife, let alone eat. Although not a lot is known about this virus, it seems to arise from the use of infected wood as a scion material when propagating. Control involves destroying the tree, and propagating its replacement from virus-free material and planting it in a different spot.

Disorders

Potassium Deficiency

Pears can suffer from a variety of mineral deficiencies including iron, magnesium, calcium and manganese. Pears need potassium for a variety of functions, including fruit development. Potassium deficiency sometimes occurs, and this is seen in stunted growth and poor fruit development, and older leaves having scorched leaf margins. The remedy is the application of a potassium-rich general fertiliser in spring to the soil around the base of the tree.

Pests

Pear Bedstraw Aphid

Pear bedstraw aphid is seen on pear foliage in early summer. The small pink/grey aphids are seen feeding in large numbers on young shoots. Like many aphids, the population increases quickly by asexual reproduction (parthenogenesis), and the colonies can become very dense. The sucking of sap from the leaves causes them to curl inwards, and ant activity is a common indicator of the aphids' presence. Aphids feed on amino acids in the plant sap, and abort sugar. This sugar solution (honeydew) lands on lower leaves and turns black as it is digested by fungi (sooty moulds). Ants feed on the sugar solution and form a symbiotic relationship with the aphids, and will defend them against their predators such as ladybirds.

In midsummer the aphid moves to its summer host, weeds, and cultivated plants of the genus *Galium*, which include the woodruffs and the common weed cleavers (*Galium aparine*). In autumn the aphids return to pear trees, where they overwinter.

Heavy infestations of the aphid will stunt the growth of the tree, but fortunately they have many predators that are prepared to do battle with the ants to get to their prey. Ladybirds, ground beetles, parasitoid wasps and earwigs are all good predators of aphids, as are several species of bird.

If the infestation of this pest is not too great, there is a lot of justification for allowing nature to take its course and to allow the predators to reduce the population to an acceptable level. Small, localised populations can be controlled by squashing the aphids between thumb and forefinger, or snipping off the affected growth.

Using pesticides to control aphids may not be the best approach, as the rapid rate of breeding can result in the rapid development of populations that are resistant to a particular pesticide. Naturally occurring plant oils formulated for aphid control can give satisfactory results. These products are usually combined with a growth enhancer to mitigate the effects of the aphids. A plant-oil-based winter wash will help to kill overwintering eggs of these and other aphids.

Pear Blister Mite

This pest can cause alarm but seldom does sufficient damage to cause concern. The symptoms are yellowish-green blisters that appear in early summer. These blisters can be up to 4mm (0.157in) in diameter. As the season progresses, the affected areas turn black, and this can affect large proportions of the leaf. The damage is caused by a microscopic mite that lives inside the foliage during the growing season and moves to the bud scales to overwinter. The symptoms of this pest may be confused with pear scab, which is more damaging.

Pear leaf blister mite. This pest looks serious, but it has little effect on cropping. Pulling off the affected leaves is likely to do more harm than good.

Codling Moth

More commonly seen on apples, codling moths can also attack pears, leading to maggoty fruit. When affected fruits are cut open, the feeding damage can be seen as well as the caterpillar's excrement (frass). Affected fruits may ripen and fall prematurely. If the pest population is low, the level of damage to the crop can be tolerated, but if attacks are more serious, additional control measures may be warranted. Natural predators such as blue tits and earwigs should be encouraged as they will eat the eggs of codling moths, and codling moth traps may be used.

Codling moth traps are based on a sex attractant used by the female moth to attract a mate, and these traps are available to amateur gardeners. They are used widely by commercial growers to monitor the population of this pest to see whether it reaches the threshold that warrants the use of pesticides or biological control measures. For amateur growers, the traps may provide sufficient control of male codling moths to reduce caterpillar damage to an acceptable level. The traps are placed in the branches of the trees in early May in readiness for the adults to emerge later on that month and for the females to lay eggs near developing fruitlets. After hatching, the caterpillars bore into the fruitlets and feed inside them for about a month. They will overwinter in leaf litter or in bark crevices.

A pathogenic nematode (eelworm) can be used to control codling moth. A solution containing live nematodes is sprayed on to the bark in early autumn to kill the caterpillars that have left the fruitlets and are preparing to overwinter. Nematode treatment does not prevent codling moth adults coming from outside the garden or orchard in late spring, so it is unlikely to be effective if there are orchards nearby. Chemical control using an approved pesticide should only be used if the traps indicate a high codling moth population. Trees in flower must never be sprayed with pesticide, to prevent poisoning the pollinators.

Slugworm

Pear and cherry slugworm is in the same insect order as bees, wasps and sawflies. The larvae of this insect resemble small black slugs and grow to about 1cm (0.4in) in length. The larvae feed on the upper side of the foliage, and affected areas turn brown. Usually this pest does not cause sufficient damage to warrant control measures. There are usually three generations of this pest, and when they have matured, larvae fall to the ground and overwinter there before emerging as adults the following spring.

Pear Midge

Pear midge is a potentially serious pest of pears and may result in the loss of the entire crop. The small larvae eat the fruitlets from inside, which causes affected fruitlets to drop in June. The first sign that

Codling moth traps are used by both amateur and professional growers: by emitting the pheromone emitted by the female moth, males are attracted and become trapped.

something is wrong is that some fruitlets start to expand at a faster rate than others and start to turn black at the eye end in May. The blackening of the fruitlet continues in June, and it drops off. Cutting open the fruitlet will reveal the presence of orange-white larvae about 4mm (¼in) long. Adult pear midges are small flies, and after mating, the females lay their eggs in unopened pear blossom. The larvae eat the centres of the flowers and feed inside the developing fruitlets. By June, the larvae have finished feeding and overwinter in the soil before pupating and emerging as adults in spring. The severity of infestations will be variable. In some years they will not cause significant damage, but monitoring is essential.

Pulling off and destroying infected fruitlets will not prevent damage to the current crop but it will reduce the pest population for the following year. If the tree is growing in bare soil, hoeing round the base of the tree may help to kill overwintering larvae; if the tree is growing in grass, scarifying the grass in winter could have the same effect. Scattering some bird seed round the base of the tree might encourage birds to feed on the larvae of this pest and those of codling moth and slugworm.

Following a severe attack of pear midge during the previous year, the use of a pesticide may be justified. Plant-oil or fatty-acid pesticides are much safer for the environment than their synthetic counterparts. Spraying is carried out before the blossoms open at the 'white bud' stage when the adults are laying their eggs.

Birds

Birds are just as big a pest of pears as they are of apples, and the same control measures can be employed (*see* Chapter 3: Growing Apples).

Pruning and Training

The similarity between apples and pears means that pear trees can be pruned and trained in the same way as apples. Please refer to the Pruning and Training section in Chapter 3: Growing Apples.

Thinning

Pears are generally thinned to one fruit per cluster for larger-fruited varieties such as Beurre Hardy, but this could be increased to two for smaller-fruited ones such as Beth. Excess, very small and deformed fruits are removed after the June drop.

Watering and Feeding

Pear trees may need watering for the first eighteen months after planting, with water being applied thoroughly but with enough time for it to drain between repeat waterings. A weekly soak is much better than a daily dribble, which will encourage shallow rooting. Allowing the roots to grow down in search of water promotes deep rooting. Established trees may benefit from watering during periods of drought, but as more attention becomes focused on conserving water as a valuable resource, this may be hard to justify. Mulching trees when the soil is moist in spring will help to conserve summer moisture.

Pears need potassium to promote flowering and fruiting, so the application of a high-potassium general fertiliser is ideal for them. This is best applied when growth commences in spring.

Harvesting and Storage

European pears are best picked slightly underripe and will continue to ripen in storage. Asian pears are best picked fully ripe as they will not ripen further after picking. The fruits should detach easily from the tree with a gentle twist.

Early pears such as Williams' Bon Chrétien have poor storage qualities and will rot very quickly; they should be inspected daily and rotting fruit removed immediately. European pears with good keeping qualities such as Winter Nelis can be stored like apples in a cool, frost-free location that is protected from mice.

CHAPTER 5

GROWING PLUMS

Plums are a diverse group of fruits all belonging to the genus *Prunus*, which includes cherries, plums, peaches and apricots. Cultivated European plums originated in eastern Europe, the Caucasus, Anatolia and Iran, and are mainly variants of *Prunus domestica* including gages, damsons, bullaces and mirabelles. Chinese plums – incorrectly known as Japanese plums – are varieties of *Prunus salicina* and a few other species, and are the most widely cultivated type of plum on account of their comparatively long storage qualities. European plums may lack the storage properties of their Chinese counterparts but have a better flavour.

Gages (*Prunus domestica* subspecies *Italica*) are considered to be the best flavoured plums; they are believed to have originated in Iran and were imported to Britain via France by Sir William Gage. Gages are sometimes called greengages, but as not all of them are green, I have used the name 'gage' rather than separating greengages from the other ones. Gages are small spherical plums with an exquisitely sweet flavour. They are generally less reliable than ordinary plums, but this is a small price to pay for their sheer opulence: they are pure confectionery.

Ordinary or prune plums make up the majority of varieties. They are usually oval shaped and are available in a variety of colours from blue to red and yellow. Most are suitable for cooking or for eating fresh. The popular variety Victoria typifies this group, and the fruit can be enjoyed fresh or made into a variety of delicious desserts and conserves. The term 'prune plum' is used mainly in the United States as these plums can be dried to make prunes, whereas their Chinese counterparts cannot be dried easily owing to their high juice content.

Damsons (*Prunus domestica* subspecies *Insititia*) are generally smaller and more astringent than prune plums. The variety Merryweather is sweet enough to be eaten fresh when allowed to ripen fully on the tree, however most other varieties need cooking and a little sweetening. They are excellent for making pies, tarts and conserves. Damson wine is a highly rated 'hedgerow' wine. Damsons are considered to originate from Damascus.

Bullaces are small round plums and may actually be native. They are often found growing wild in hedgerows, and there are a few varieties that are cultivated, such as Langley. They are used primarily for cooking as they are not usually sweet enough to eat fresh.

Mirabelles are a small type of plum that is believed to have originated in Anatolia. They are sweet and versatile and are becoming increasingly popular in Britain.

Cherry plums (*Prunus cerasifera*) are small plums resembling large cherries. They are usually grown from seed by nurseries for use as hedging plants. They can therefore be used to make an excellent and productive

Prunus cerasifera 'Princess' is both productive and very ornamental.

hedge. There are some ornamental varieties of cherry plum such as *Prunus cerasifera* 'Pissardii' (purple-leaved plum) and *Prunus cerasifera* 'Princess' with its impressive flowering display. Both these ornamental varieties can bear fruit.

Plums are early flowering and are best planted in areas protected from spring frosts. Damsons are wind resistant and have been used as windbreaks in orchards. They are excellent for use in exposed places where other plums may fail.

Selected Varieties

As with all fruits, endeavours are being made all over the world to bring new varieties of plum to gardeners and commercial growers. Alternatives to the excellent but disease-prone variety Victoria have been developed, as well as those that display resistance to the serious virus disease Sharka.

Ordinary or Prune Plums

Plum Czar – frost-resistant and partially self-fertile.

Plum Jubilee – similar to Victoria but it ripens a week earlier and has larger fruit.

Plum Victoria – the most popular plum grown in the UK. It is versatile and heavy-cropping, but rather prone to disease.

Plum Rivers Early Prolific – a cooking plum that is self-fertile and is heavy-cropping.

Plum Marjorie's Seedling – a late-cropping, reliable variety that is suitable for eating fresh or for cooking.

Plum Opal – an excellent self-fertile plum that is rather similar to Victoria and like that variety is dual-purpose.

Plum Warwickshire Drooper – named after the drooping habit of the tree, this plum has small fruits suitable for cooking or eating fresh.

Avalon

The varieties with names based on the Arthurian legend are the product of breeding work conducted at the Long Aston Research Station near Bristol. Avalon is a popular dual-purpose self-fertile variety with large red fruits flushed with yellow. The stones separate easily from the sweet flesh. The growth is strong, and is best moderated by a dwarfing rootstock such as Pixie or VVA. The fruit is harvested in August. Pollination group 2.

Blue Tit

A dark blue self-fertile dual-purpose plum with yellow flesh. The growth is naturally compact, making it a good choice for a small garden. The flavour is pleasant but not overly sweet; the fruit must be allowed to ripen fully before picking. Harvest in August. Pollination group 2.

Czar

Czar is a popular cooking plum with a compact habit. The dark purple fruits are picked in August and have yellow flesh with a good flavour but moderate sweetness, although this plum is sometimes classified as being suitable for eating fresh. Self-fertile, pollination group 3.

Excalibur

Excalibur is an excellent sweet plum for eating fresh. The cropping is a somewhat moderate, but for gardeners this is seldom an issue as the quality of the fruit is outstanding and there is often little use for surplus fruit. The fruits are red-purple and very sweet. Growth is vigorous. It is harvested in August. Pollination group 2.

Guinevere

Guinevere is an excellent late-fruiting eating plum that ripens in September. The purple-skinned fruits have sweet yellow flesh with a good flavour. Cropping is heavy. This variety has good disease resistance. Self-fertile, pollination group 3.

Haganta

Haganta is a self-fertile late-fruiting plum from Germany with a lot of attributes. The large blue plums are very sweet for eating fresh, but it is a good cooking variety as well. The fruit will also store well, and may keep to November if refrigerated. This variety was bred for disease resistance, particularly to Sharka, the serious virus disease of stone fruits. Pollination group 3.

Jubilee

Also known as Jubileum, Jubilee is a Swedish eating variety to rival the ever-popular but disease-prone Victoria. Ripening one week before Victoria, it has larger, dark red fruits with yellow flesh with an excellent flavour. The stone separates easily from the flesh. Like Victoria, it is a vigorous grower, and this vigour is best controlled using a dwarfing rootstock such as Pixie or VVA. This variety is self-fertile and belongs in pollination group 3.

Kirkes

Kirkes is a heritage variety of eating plum grown for its superior flavour. The dark purple fruits have a richly flavoured greenish-yellow flesh. It is sometimes listed as Kirkes Blue by nurseries. Pollination group 3.

Lancelot

Lancelot is an excellent eating plum that is harvested in late August, just after Victoria. It is self-fertile and in pollination group 3.

Laxton's Delicious

A dual-purpose plum with beautiful, delicious pink fruit with yellow flesh. The fruit is picked in September. The variety is self-fertile and is in pollination group 3.

Marjorie's Seedling

Marjorie's Seedling is a late dual-purpose plum that remains popular despite newer varieties becoming available with the same cropping period. The large, purple plums are tasty, but there are sweeter alternatives such as Haganta and Guinevere. This variety is late flowering and in pollination group 5, an advantage in areas troubled by late spring frosts but a possible disadvantage if finding a pollination partner flowering equally late. Fortunately, this variety is self-fertile.

Opal

Opal is an early-eating plum that ripens in July before Victoria. It is renowned for its reliability and quality. The reddish-purple fruits have yellow flesh, from which the stone separates easily. The variety is self-fertile and is in pollination group 3.

Purple Pershore

Purple Pershore is primarily a cooking variety with reddish-purple fruits with a rich flavour. Cropping is dependable, and it is a good choice for areas troubled by spring frosts. This variety is self-fertile and is in pollination group 3.

Rivers Early Prolific

Rivers Early Prolific is a popular early plum with small purple fruits with yellow flesh; it is ready to be picked in July. The flavour is excellent, and the fruits are juicy. Cropping is good and dependable. The plums are good for eating fresh or for cooking. This variety is self-fertile and in pollination group 2.

Sanctus Hubertus

Sanctus Hubertus is an early-eating plum ready in early August. The fruits should be fully tree-ripened before picking to ensure they are sweet enough. The large fruits are purple blue with yellow flesh. The flavour is good, but the sweetness is moderate. The variety is self-fertile and in pollination group 3.

Severn Cross

Severn Cross is an excellent late plum, ripening in September. The large yellow fruits often have a pink flush; the flesh is yellow. Its heavy cropping makes it a favourite with commercial growers. The tree has a neat, pyramidal shape. This variety is self-fertile and is in pollination group 4.

Valor

Valor is a late fruiting variety for September picking that is grown commercially. The large purple fruits are sweet with yellow flesh, and are good for eating fresh or for cooking. This variety has some resistance to the devastating virus Sharka. Pollination group 3.

Victoria

Victoria is a dual-purpose self-fertile variety that outsells any other plum in garden centres and retail nurseries mainly because of its familiarity. It is also the variety most grown by commercial growers largely on account of its productivity. The bright red fruits have yellow flesh and ripen in August, and the fruit is juicy with a fair but not outstanding flavour. The stone separates easily from the flesh. This variety is rather prone to diseases such as plum rust, and it may be worth considering alternatives such as Jubilee. Pollination group 3.

Violetta

Violetta is a new, self-fertile variety from Sweden that has appeal for gardeners on account of its compact growth, making it a good choice if space is restricted. The blue plums have an excellent sweet flavour, and are good for cooking and eating fresh. Productivity is good. The variety is in pollination group 3.

Warwickshire Drooper

This variety gets its name from its spreading and drooping habit. The yellow plums are harvested in August and are juicy and moderately sweet. It is a good dual-purpose variety that is self-fertile; it is in pollination group 3.

Yellow Pershore

This dual-purpose variety is still widely grown commercially. It is a good variety for northern areas. The large, yellow, egg-shaped plums have juicy yellow flesh and a rich flavour. The variety is self-fertile, and is in pollination group 2.

Gages

Early Transparent Gage has yellow fruits flushed red and is a heavy and reliable cropper.

Gage Dennison's – this excellent variety is also known as Imperial Gage.

Gage Jefferson – originating from the USA, this gage is particularly good for growing in northern areas of the UK. When suitably pollinated, it is a heavy cropper.

Oullins Golden Gage – a highly rated gage with large fruit.

Cambridge Gage

Cambridge Gage is a variety for a sheltered sunny site, and in such a location it can produce reliable crops of small, yellowish-green fruits in August that are very sweet with an unmistakeable gage flavour. This variety is self-fertile; it is in pollination group 3.

Early Transparent

The fruits of Early Transparent have an attractive red flush, and the translucent skin of this variety reveals its golden flesh, which is richly flavoured, juicy, and pleasantly sweet. It is a reliable cropper. This variety is self-fertile and in pollination group 3.

Imperial Gage (Dennison's Superb)

This variety is also known and sold as 'Dennison's Superb'. It is a better choice for northern and Midland areas where varieties such as Cambridge Gage may fail. The large green fruits are moderately juicy and sweet. This variety is self-fertile and in pollination group 2.

Jefferson

Jefferson is an American heritage variety. The fruits are medium-sized and very sweet and juicy, and are ready for picking in August. It is a good choice for northern and exposed areas. The tree makes moderate growth. Pollination group 1.

Old Greengage

Old Greengage is a similar variety to Cambridge Gage and is the original gage that is believed to have originated from Armenia or Iran and travelled to Britain via Italy and France. The growth is compact, so it is useful for a restricted space. Like Cambridge Gage, it favours a warm, sheltered location. It is partially self-fertile and would benefit from another variety to pollinate it. Pollination group 3.

Oullins Golden Gage

Oullins Golden Gage is a heavy-cropping variety producing yellow fruits with a good flavour with moderate sweetness. The fruits are picked slightly underripe for cooking, but should be allowed to ripen fully for eating fresh. This variety is self-fertile and in pollination group 4.

Reine Claude de Bavay

Reine Claude de Bavay is the main variety of imported gages. The green fruits turn yellow on ripening, and they often have red speckles; the flesh is yellow. The fruit is deliciously sweet and richly flavoured. This variety is self-fertile; it is in pollination group 4.

Stella's Star

This tree has compact growth and will crop well from an early age; it is very productive. The yellow/green fruits have a mild but pleasant flavour. This variety is self-fertile and belongs in pollination group 3.

Damsons and Bullaces

Damson Farleigh – a compact damson with a rich flavour.

Damson Merryweather – the best damson for eating fresh.

Damson Shropshire Prune – a very reliable variety with a good, intense flavour.

Farleigh

The main attributes of the variety Farleigh are its hardiness, heavy cropping, and compact growth. It is a good choice for northern areas or exposed locations. The fruits that ripen in September are rather small in size, but the flavour is good. It is probably best for cooking. The variety is self-fertile and is in pollination group 3.

Langley Bullace

The small fruits of Langley Bullace ripen in October and are blue-black with a good bloom. The variety is best for culinary use as the taste is rather sharp. The variety is self-fertile and belongs in pollination group 2.

Merryweather

Merryweather is a very popular variety of damson with comparatively large blue-black fruits that are sweet enough to be eaten fresh without losing any of the characteristic damson flavour. The cropping is both heavy and reliable, and the tree makes vigorous growth and shows some resistance to silver leaf disease. The fruit ripens in September. The variety is self-fertile and belongs in pollination group 3.

Shropshire Prune

This reliable variety has intense 'wild' damson flavour and is an excellent choice for cooking. The dark blue fruits ripen in September. The variety is self-fertile and belongs in pollination group 3.

Mirabelles

Mirabelle Gypsy – this modern variety is both ornamental and productive. The delicious, sweet fruits have an attractive red skin and juicy orange flesh. The spring blossom is outstanding.

Mirabelle Ruby Columnar – this has large fruit for a Mirabelle. The fruit has a very sweet, peach-like flavour. The narrow habit of the tree makes it suitable for growing in confined spaces.

Mirabelle De Nancy. This is an excellent dual-purpose Mirabelle with rich, sweet flesh. It is good for bottling.

Countess

Countess is a new dual-purpose variety, with superb, round, dark red-purple plummy fruit with a lovely flavour. The flesh is red to yellow with a wonderful melting texture, juicy, sweet and rich in flavour. It has excellent eating quality but can also be used in cooking. It is a freestone variety: the stone comes away from the flesh when fully ripe. It has stunning white blossom in the spring. The fruit is harvested in September, and the variety is in pollination group 1.

De Nancy

De Nancy is a popular dual-purpose heritage variety from France, with orange-yellow fruits that ripen in September. The yellow flesh is very sweet, and the stone separates easily from it. The tree makes neat, pyramidal growth. Pollination group 1.

Gypsy

This modern variety from Ukraine is particularly good for eating fresh, with deliciously sweet red fruits with orange flesh. The fruits are harvested in August, and the variety belongs in pollination group 1.

Ruby Columnar

The narrow habit of this tree makes it a good choice where space is restricted. The fruit is large for a Mirabelle and has a pleasant, sweet flavour resembling a peach. The fruit is harvested in September, and the variety is in pollination group 1.

Rootstocks

As with most fruit-tree rootstocks, the ones that have the strongest dwarfing effect will result in reduced tree size and earlier cropping, but at the expense of being intolerant of poor soils, waterlogging and drought. Plums are no exception. In the United Kingdom there are four main plum rootstocks; these are suitable for growing plums, damsons, gages and mirabelles.

Pixy (Semi-Dwarfing)

This rootstock was developed by the East Malling Research Station in Kent in 1949 and came into common usage in the 1970s. It was developed from a seedling of the St Julian A rootstock. It is the main semi-dwarfing rootstock used in the UK. It is slightly more precocious than St Julian A, with cropping usually one year earlier. Plum trees grown on this rootstock usually grow to about 2.5 to 3m (8 to 10ft) in height, but this will also be governed by the natural vigour of the scion variety. Trees on this rootstock will need staking for four or five years, and permanently on exposed sites. This rootstock should only be used in good soils. It is suitable for growing plums in large containers in a loam-based growing medium.

VVA (Semi-Dwarfing)

This rootstock is becoming increasingly popular and is gradually replacing Pixy. It was developed from a hybrid of two wild plum species, *Prunus tomentosa* and *Prunus cerasifera* (cherry plum). In many ways it is similar to Pixy in terms of tree size, but it is hardier and the fruit size is better. It is very similar to the Plumina rootstock from France. Like Pixy, trees on this rootstock need staking for four or five years, and permanently on an exposed site. Good soil conditions are necessary, and trees can be planted in large containers using a loam-based growing medium.

St Julian A (Semi-Vigorous)

St Julian A is the main plum rootstock used in the UK. It is used for bush and half-standard trees as well as fans. Trees grown as bushes usually achieve a height between 3 and 3.5m (10 and 11.5ft) and so may require the use of ladders for picking. Cropping starts after about three to four years after planting. This rootstock is more tolerant of poor soils than VVA or Pixy, and trees on it need staking for two to three years.

Brompton (Very Vigorous)

Trees on this rootstock will grow in excess of 5m (16ft), so are more suited to growing in farm orchards than gardens. This rootstock is tolerant of poor soil, but trees may take a comparatively long time to come into bearing.

Like apple and pear rootstocks, plum rootstocks are usually propagated by mound layering, a process described in Chapter 3: Growing Apples.

Pollination

Most plum varieties can be classified in five pollination groups, with most varieties belonging to groups 2, 3 and 4. Many varieties such as Victoria are reliably self-fertile, others are partially self-fertile, but a significant number are self-sterile and need a compatible pollinator belonging to the same or an adjacent pollination group.

Plums are very early flowering and blossoms are liable to spring frost damage. Trees grown on dwarfing rootstocks such as Pixy or VVA and trained trees can be protected from frost damage using horticultural fleece.

The late-flowering variety Marjorie's Seedling is an excellent choice for gardens where late spring frosts can be troublesome.

Diseases, Disorders and Pests

Diseases

Silver Leaf

Silver leaf is a potentially serious fungal disease that can prove fatal for plums and other stone fruits. It may also affect apples, rhododendron and laburnum, but this is less common. It is sometimes mistaken for false silver leaf, a physiological disorder that may be caused by unfavourable weather conditions rather than a pathogenic fungus. The fungus causing silver leaf disease, *Chrondostereum purpureum*, makes the tissues in the leaves separate, causing a silvering of the foliage even though it does not infect the foliage. Infected shoots die back, and there is a characteristic staining of the wood beneath the bark.

The fungus produces its most infectious spores during winter, and these can enter the wood via pruning cuts and broken branches and other wounds. It is essential not to prune plums or other susceptible plants during the winter months. Pruning must be carried out during the warmer months (months without an R in them), and do not be put off by the fact that the tree will be carrying developing fruit during the pruning period. In summer there are fewer infectious spores, and pruning wounds seal over quickly, minimising the chances of infection.

Infections of silver leaf must be dealt with quickly by cutting out infected wood with a clean, sterilised pruning saw. The cuts must be made at least 15cm (6in) beyond the infected wood; the extent of infection is

Silver leaf is a serious fungal disease of plum and other stone fruits. To avoid the risk of infection, trees should be pruned only in the summer months and pruning tools regularly sterilised.

indicated by the staining. The pruning saw will need to be sterilised after each cut using a horticultural sterilant or methylated spirits. The infected wood must be taken off site or burned. The fungus is capable of living as spores on dead wood, so timely destruction or removal of infected wood is essential. The variety Victoria is rather prone to infection by silver leaf disease.

Rust

Plum rust is a relatively minor disease of plums; it may reduce the size of the crop and the sugar content of the fruit, but is seldom serious enough to cause major problems. The symptoms of the disease are yellow-green lesions on the upper surface of the foliage, with brown raised pustules on the corresponding lower surfaces of the leaves. The brown pustules release spores that spread infection. Small longitudinal cankers can appear on infected wood, and fruit can be infected, showing brown spots with yellow-green 'haloes'. Infected leaves will fall prematurely. As with several diseases of plum, the variety Victoria is rather susceptible. As with most rusts, there is an alternative host – in the case of plum rust it is anemones.

Control of this disease is not easy; raking up fallen leaves may reduce infection, and annual feed will promote new growth to mitigate the effects of the disease. There are no chemical control products available to amateur gardeners.

Bacterial Canker

Bacterial canker is quite a common disease of plums, cherries and all species belonging to the genus *Prunus*. It is caused by two closely related species of bacteria. The symptoms of this disease are small, sunken patches of dead bark and leaves with many small holes in them (bacterial shot hole disease). Affected wood may ooze gum, but this can also be caused by other factors. There is no chemical control for this disease: cankers need to be cut out using sterilised pruning equipment. Pruning is best conducted in July when the natural resistance to this pathogen is greatest. Prunings should be burned or taken off site.

The plum varieties Marjorie's Seedling and Warwickshire Drooper have some natural resistance to this disease.

Pocket Plum

Pocket plum is a fungal disease of plums that is closely related to, but less serious than, peach leaf-curl disease of peaches, almonds and apricots. Distorted plums without stones appear from midsummer onwards. These are inedible. There may be some distortion of shoots, and 'witches brooms', which are a congested mass of live and dead shoots, may appear on the branches. Shoots bearing distorted fruits and abnormal growths should be removed to provide effective control of this disease. There is no available chemical control.

Sharka (Plum Pox)

Fortunately Sharka is a very rare viral disease, but it is mentioned as it poses a serious threat to plums. The disease was discovered in Bulgaria in 1917 and has spread to most plum-growing regions in the world since then. It is spread by aphids feeding on the trees and the use of infected graft wood for propagation. Despite strict control measures, the disease entered the UK and its spread is being monitored carefully. The disease can infect wild plum species such as the sloe (*Prunus spinosa*), making control difficult.

The symptoms of this disease can vary greatly according to the variety and season, with infections developing slowly at first, affecting a few branches initially. Leaves may develop yellow spots, and fruits may become spotted with sunken areas. Affected fruit has a sour taste and is inedible. The seriousness of this disease means that suspected outbreaks in the UK should be reported to the local plant health inspectorate, and if it is a confirmed case of Sharka, the tree must be destroyed immediately. The plum variety Haganta has good resistance to Sharka.

Powdery Mildew

Powdery mildew of plum is less common and serious than its counterpart in apples. Powdery mildews are very host-specific, so powdery mildew of plum will not affect apple trees, and vice versa. The symptoms of this disease are a white powdery deposit on the foliage. Like all fungal pathogens, powdery mildew will weaken the tree, which will have an effect on cropping. The best prevention is to prune the tree to allow good air circulation between the branches, and to remove fallen leaves in autumn. Mulching the trees in spring will help to conserve soil moisture in summer and reduce the severity of the disease.

Brown Rot

Brown rot is caused by the same two species of fungi causing brown rot in apples and pears. It tends to be more serious in plums, and may ruin an entire crop. Fruits turn brown and rotten, often with concentric rings of pustules on the surface of the fruit. This is particularly apparent in wet weather. Fruits may fall, or shrivel and remain on the tree. The same fungi cause blossom rot, in which blossoms turn brown and die. Small cankers may become visible on affected shoots.

Fruits that have been damaged are most prone to attack, so controlling bird damage by netting or other techniques will help to reduce brown rot. Infection can spread from one damaged fruit to other fruits in a cluster, so rapid removal of rotten fruits is essential to minimise the effects of this disease. Removal of fallen fruits can reduce incidence of this disease, but the fruits will have to be taken away from the trees to avoid reinfection. The fungus overwinters on cankers and on infected fruit, which then infects the blossoms before moving on to damaged fruit.

Disorders

Split Fruit

Plums are prone to splitting when the tree receives an erratic water supply. This is particularly common when a long period of drought is followed by heavy rainfall. The use of organic mulches around the base of the tree in spring will help to conserve moisture and minimise the incidence of fruit splitting.

Pests

Aphids

There are two species of aphid that are commonly seen on plums. The plum leaf-curling aphid is often seen in the early part of the season in April and May. It is evidenced by young leaves curling inwards, and there is often ant activity on affected shoots. The mealy plum aphid is seen later on, when colonies of this grey insect can be seen on the undersides of leaves. The mealy plum aphid causes no leaf distortion, but as the aphids feed on the leaf sap, they abort unwanted sugar in liquid form, and this falls on lower leaves where it is consumed by fungi, resulting in black 'sooty moulds'. Ants relish this sugar solution and are often seen amongst the aphid colonies.

There is no doubt that aphids feeding on the sap weakens the trees, but in most cases, the cost of controlling aphids is seldom justified. Aphids have a host of natural enemies including ladybirds, lacewings, hoverflies and wasps. However, in young trees, aphid attacks can be quite damaging, and spraying is not difficult. There are several good insecticides for aphid control based on naturally occurring substances such as plant oils and fatty acids, and these provide an effective and environmentally safe form of control.

The leaf-curling plum aphid is commonly seen on plum trees. Control may be necessary on young trees, but this pest seldom does much damage on established ones.

Spotted Wing Drosophila (SWD)

SWD is a potentially serious pest that was first seen in Britain in 2012. The pest attacks stone fruit and soft fruits. The species originated in Asia and is a relative of the fruit flies that can turn fruit juices or wine into vinegar. They can also make their annoying presence felt near bowls of ripe fruit. The spotted wing drosophila, unlike our native fruit flies, can attack underripe fruit using a serrated ovipositor to break the skin of the ripening fruit, and will then lay its eggs inside the flesh. The eggs then hatch, and the larvae, which grow to about 4mm (¼in), consume the fruit, making it unusable. Being an unwelcome visitor, the pest does not have natural enemies to control its population, and insecticides are ineffective.

Scientists all over the world are trying to develop control measures for this serious pest. The two main control measures are trapping using a liquid bait and the use of ultrafine mesh (0.9mm) to prevent the pest reaching the crop. Unfortunately, this pest can overwinter in the UK and feed on the fruits of a variety of native plants including blackberry and sloe, resulting in populations of spotted wing drosophila that can move on to cultivated fruits. It is hoped that the research into control measures for this pest will produce results. The pest can be identified using a hand lens by the presence of the serrated ovipositor on females and the spotted wings on males.

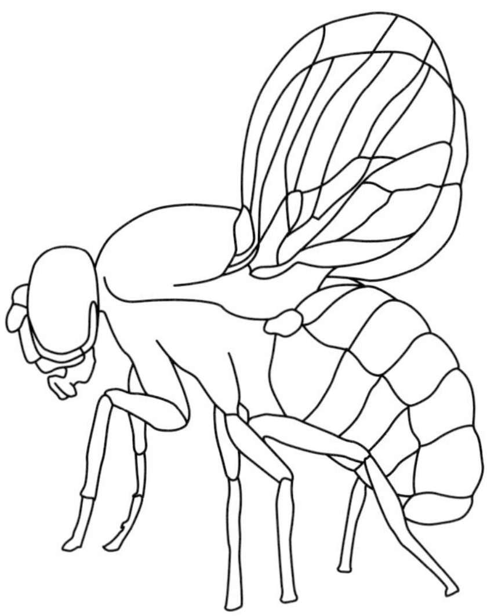

Spotted wing drosophila.

Affected fruits must not be composted as composting will draw in a greater number of the pests. The affected fruit should be placed in a very well-sealed black polythene bag and allowed to heat up in the sun to kill the flies.

Plum Sawfly

There are two distinct pests called plum sawfly, which can be rather confusing. Fortunately, neither poses a serious threat to plum trees, and control is seldom worth the time and trouble. The olive green or black larvae of *Caliroa cerasi* feed on the foliage of plums and related species including apple. The leaves may become skeletonised, and heavy infestations on young trees can be controlled by a fatty-acid contact insecticide. The larvae of the other sawfly, *Hoplocampa flava*, feed on fruitlets early in the season. A single larva will feed on about four fruitlets before dropping to the ground to pupate. The affected fruitlets drop to the ground without developing, though the loss of fruit is usually minimal. In fact the fruit-eating sawfly is usually a beneficial thinning agent, and so control is seldom justified.

Plum Moth

Plum moth is the cause of maggoty ripe fruits. The larvae of this pest feed with the fruits, they are pink with a brown head and grow up to 12mm (½in) in length. Affected fruits become misshapen and ripen prematurely, and when the fruit is cut open, small brown pellets of excrement can be seen. As affected fruits ripen early, it is possible to overestimate the size of the pest problem as fruits ripening later will have fewer larvae. In many seasons, the loss of the crop due to plum moth is likely to be tolerable, and no control measures are warranted.

Pheromone traps similar to those used for monitoring codling moth of apple are used to monitor plum moth. These are readily available from specialist suppliers and garden centres, and are hung in the trees in early May to attract male moths. The moths are trapped on a sticky surface on the base of the trap, which should be designed so as not to trap birds. Large populations of this pest appearing in the traps indicate the need for additional control measures. The instructions supplied with the traps should indicate the thresholds for taking additional control measures and their timings.

If deemed necessary, insecticidal sprays should be applied around the third week in June, with possibly a second spray about three weeks later. The environmental impact of using an insecticide must be considered; insecticides based on natural products such as Pyrethrum or acetic acid will have little environmental impact but will have a low persistence and may need repeat sprays to be effective.

The larvae leave the fruits in late summer to early autumn and overwinter in bark crevices. At this time they are vulnerable to attack by pathogenic nematodes, which are available from specialist suppliers. A suspension of nematodes is sprayed on to the trunk and branches, and the soil beneath the canopy of the tree. Nematode treatment will help to kill overwintering populations in the vicinity of the tree, but will not stop adults flying in from other areas, so it may not be effective in areas where there are a lot of plum trees.

Birds and Wasps

Birds and wasps attack all top fruits, and their control is mentioned in the Pests section in Chapter 3: Growing Apples.

Pruning and Training

Plums generally require less pruning than apples and pears, and two potentially serious diseases – namely silver leaf and bacterial canker – can infect trees via pruning cuts. It is important to minimise infections by restricting the number of pruning cuts, and to do the work in summer so that pruning wounds can heal quickly.

Plums are usually grown as bush trees in the open and fan-trained trees against sunny walls. Wall culture is useful for many gages, such as Cambridge Gage, that appreciate the warm microclimate of a south- or west-facing wall, and also because fleece can be used for spring frost protection and mesh to protect the fruits from birds and the spotted wing drosophila.

Where a larger tree is required, standard and half-standard trees grown on vigorous rootstocks such as Brompton are useful, but tree management including harvesting and pruning will inevitably require the use of ladders.

Where space is very limited, it is possible to grow plums as cordons or pyramids. When grown on a dwarfing rootstock such trees are easily managed and can be sprayed, pruned, and covered by fleece or protective netting.

It is a good idea to sterilise saws and secateurs when moving from one plum tree to another to minimise the risk of silver leaf infection.

Bush Trees

The formative pruning of plum trees is the same as that for apples, except that the formative pruning cuts are made in early spring rather than in winter. Once the framework of branches has been established, the maintenance pruning cuts are made in summer. Pruning bush plums aims to achieve an open goblet shape and in doing so to remove crossing, dead, diseased and rubbing growths.

Pyramid Trees

Pyramid plums have the advantage of taking up less space than their bush counterparts. They are best grown on moderately vigorous rootstocks such as VVA or St Julian A. They need staking: trees on a dwarfing rootstock need a stake 1.8m (6ft) tall, and those on the St Julian A or similar rootstock need one that is 2.4m (8ft) tall. The stake is permanent and so should be treated against decay.

Starting with an unfeathered maiden (a one-year-old tree consisting of a single shoot with no side growths), a cut is made just above a bud to stimulate side branches. For trees on a dwarfing rootstock such as VVA or Pixy, this cut is made 60cm (24in) from the ground; for trees on St Julian A, the cut should be made about 75cm (30in) from the ground.

In the following spring the leading shoot is tied to the stake and shortened by a third. Approximately four well-spaced side branches should be selected to make the framework of the tree. These are shortened by half to encourage lateral growth.

In late July of the following year, the branch leaders are shortened to 20cm (8in) and the side branches to

15cm (6in); when the central leader reaches the top of the stake, it is shortened to about 20cm (7–8in).

Fan-Trained Plums

Fan-trained plums are created in the same way as the process described in Chapter 3: Growing Apples, except that the work is carried out in spring for formative pruning and in summer for maintenance pruning. Unless the available space is large, fan-trained plums need to be grown on a dwarfing or St Julian A rootstock. On a Pixy rootstock a fan-trained plum can be expected to cover an area 2m (6.5ft) high and 4.5m (15ft) wide, while on St Julian A, the area covered would be about 2.4m (8ft) high and 5.5m (18ft) wide. The vigour of the scion variety will have some influence on these dimensions.

Thinning

Plums are very prone to overcropping especially if spring frosts and plum sawfly have failed to reduce the number of developing fruitlets. As tempting as it may be, allowing all the fruits to develop in a year of heavy set can result in serious branch breakage, and worse still, can create points of entry for the potentially fatal silver leaf disease. In late May or early June, the developing fruits will need to be thinned so that they are about 5 to 8cm (2 to 3in) apart. This will mean taking off most of the fruitlets when there are heavily laden clusters. As well as reducing the risk of branch breakage, fruit thinning will also reduce the incidence of brown rot by increasing the spacings between fruits. Fruits can be removed by thumb or forefinger, but the thin blades of garden snips make the task a lot easier. Any fruit developing on a plum tree during its first year of growth should be removed to allow the tree to establish properly.

Watering and Feeding

A newly planted tree will require watering in dry periods for its first year. As with most plants, the best method is to water thoroughly but infrequently. A weekly bucket of water will do more good than a daily sprinkling with a hose. An organic mulch applied to the soil when planting and then applied annually in spring helps to conserve soil moisture in summer. Well-rotted farmyard manure or garden compost will perform two functions: firstly to function as a mulch, and secondly to supply plant nutrients. Alternatively, a granular balanced fertiliser containing roughly equal proportions of the three main plant nutrients, nitrogen, phosphorus and potassium, can be applied at the approved rate as soon as growth commences in spring. Extra care needs to be taken when growing trees on the VVA or Pixy rootstock as these trees will need more diligent watering and feeding.

Harvesting and Storage

Plums need to be picked as soon as they start to soften. Some varieties, such as Marjorie's Seedling, need to be tree-ripened as late as possible to maximise the sweetness of the fruit. Unlike apples, plums cannot be stored for a long time and are best used as fresh as possible. It is possible to extend the useful life of fresh plums by storing them in a refrigerator. Large trees will produce too many fruits for even a large household, and this is why small trees on dwarfing rootstocks are so valuable. Excess fruit that cannot be sold or given away can be made into delicious conserves, or bottled for later use. It pays to have a plan to deal with these surplus fruits. Damsons make an excellent hedgerow wine, or can be infused in gin or vodka to make a welcome winter drink. It is possible to freeze plums for later use after they have been stoned.

CHAPTER 6

GROWING CHERRIES

In commercial horticulture in the United Kingdom cherries have become the most widely grown stone fruit, replacing plums. The reasons for this are the development of new varieties suitable for the British climate, and rootstocks that moderate growth to allow easy management of the trees. These developments have favoured the amateur grower for the same reasons. Before these new developments, sweet cherries were grown on rootstocks that resulted in trees that grew more than 10m (30ft) in height, and selecting pollinators for these trees was an absolute nightmare. Most sweet cherry varieties at the time were self-sterile, and within the pollination groups there were many instances of incompatibility. Trees on vigorous rootstocks take a comparatively long time to come into bearing and their ultimate size meant that pruning was difficult and harvesting hazardous.

Many modern sweet cherry varieties are self-fertile, and the Gisela 5 rootstock can produce trees that are small enough to be grown in containers on the patio or in a polythene tunnel. Small trees can be netted to protect the fruits from birds, whereas the large trees of old orchards had to resort to noisy bird scarers working constantly throughout daylight hours, something that a home gardener would probably not be able to use without upsetting the neighbours.

Cherries are divided into two main groups: sweet cherries developed from *Prunus avium*, and sour cherries from *Prunus cerasus*. Sweet cherries are believed to have originated in Asia Minor in the fertile lands between the Black Sea and the Caspian Sea. The spread westwards from their point of origin was most probably facilitated by birds. The Greeks cultivated cherries, and the fruit migrated westwards. It is believed that cherry cultivation in Britain was started by the Romans, but it received a boost under the reign of Henry VIII, who imported varieties from France for his orchards in Kent. Cherry trees were exported to the United Sates in the seventeenth century by Dutch and British settlers. The sour cherry, *Prunus cerasus*, is believed to have originated in Eastern Europe. Although not sweet enough to be eaten fresh, the sour cherry is a valued ingredient for pies and jams, and makes a small, easily managed tree that can even be grown against a north-facing wall.

Cherries are grown all over the world, with the largest producer currently being Turkey. They need cool winters and dry summers, and the delicate fruits are easily spoiled by summer rain and hail. Commercial cherry production in the UK is carried out from Kent to Scotland, with dwarf trees being grown under polythene tunnels to protect the flowers from frost and the fruit from hail and rain.

Although there are many heritage varieties dating back to the nineteenth century, most commercial and amateur production in the UK uses modern varieties with good disease resistance; these were developed in Canada.

Selected Varieties

Cherry Amber Heart – a very popular variety. It ripens in mid-July.

Cherry Athos – a popular dwarf cherry that is useful where space is restricted.

Cherry Lapin – this variety produces heavy crops of dark red sweet fruits. It is self-fertile.

Cherry Morello – the most popular acid cherry. It can be grown on a north-facing wall.

Cherry Napoleon Bigarreau – despite its name, this variety originates from Germany. The white fruits have attractive red marbling and a good balance of sweetness and acidity.

Cherry Van – a dark-skinned cherry with an excellent flavour. It needs a pollinator to set fruit.

Cherry Stella – produces large, high-quality fruits but can be prone to splitting.

Cherry Merton Glory – one of the best early cherry varieties with large white fruits flushed red.

Amber Heart

Amber Heart is a popular Kent-raised variety with pink skin and yellow flesh. The fruits have a sweet flavour and ripen in mid-July. The tree has a compact habit, making it a good choice for restricted spaces. This variety requires a pollinator such as Celeste, Lapins Cherokee, Stella, Sunburst or Waterloo.

Athos

Athos is an unusual cherry and one of the 'Musketeer' varieties bred in Canada. It is unusual as it is grown as a dwarf bush usually on its own roots, rather than being grafted on to a rootstock. It is capable of producing good crops of dark red cherries that have a good balance of sweetness and acidity in mid-July. This variety is self-fertile. There are two other Musketeer cherries with similar characteristics: Porthos and Aramis. All the Musketeer cherries are suitable for growing in containers, and on their own roots will achieve an ultimate height of about 2m (6.5ft).

Celeste

Celeste is another cherry variety with compact growth, and being self-fertile is a good choice for garden cultivation, including growing in containers. The dark red fruits are very sweet and ripen in mid-July.

Christiana

The main feature of Christiana is its comparatively long cropping period. The sweet, dark red fruits are ripe in about mid-July. This variety requires a pollinator such as Celeste, Lapins Cherokee, Sunburst, Stella or Waterloo.

Kordia

Kordia is a late-fruiting black cherry that is reliable and heavy-cropping, and has found favour with both amateur and professional growers. The fruits have a good acidity and sugar balance. This variety is resistant to fruit splitting so is a good choice for high rainfall areas. The fruit ripens in late August. This variety requires a pollinator such as Celeste, Lapins Cherokee, Stella, Sunburst or Waterloo.

Lapins Cherokee

The cherry Lapins Cherokee was one of the first modern self-fertile varieties from Canada, and like Kordia, it is resistant to fruit splitting. The fruit ripens in mid-July.

Merton Glory

The large, heart-shaped fruits are pale yellow with a red flush and ripen in mid-July. This variety requires a pollinator such as Celeste, Lapins Cherokee, Stella, Sunburst or Waterloo.

Meteor Korai

The outstanding features of the variety Meteor Korai are that the dark red fruits ripen early in mid-June, and it is a 'Duke' cherry, which is a cross between a sweet and sour cherry, making it dual-purpose. It is naturally very compact, making it a great choice for garden cultivation, especially as it is self-fertile.

Morello

Morello is by far the most popular acid cherry. It can be grown in partial shade, and as a fan-trained tree can be grown against a north-facing wall. The dark red fruits ripen in mid-July but should be left on the tree for as long as possible to develop maximum sweetness. The bittersweet fruit is highly prized by cooks. Being moderately vigorous, this cherry is good for confined spaces.

Napoleon Bigarreau

The large, heart-shaped fruits of Napoleon Bigarreau are pale yellow with a red flush. The flavour is intense, with a good balance of sweetness and acidity. The fruits ripen in mid-July. This variety requires a pollinator such as Celeste, Lapins Cherokee, Stella, Sunburst or Waterloo.

Penny

Penny is an excellent late variety that is popular with commercial growers. The dark red, sweet and juicy fruits are ripe in late August. This variety requires a pollinator such as Celeste, Lapins Cherokee, Stella, Sunburst or Waterloo.

Petit Noir

Petit Noir is a late variety that ripens at the end of August. The well-flavoured fruits are dark red, and the tree makes moderate, compact growth. It is self-fertile. It is an excellent choice for garden culture and is suitable for container growing.

Stella

Stella is probably the most widely grown sweet cherry variety in the UK by both amateur and professional growers. The sweet, dark-skinned juicy fruits are produced in abundance in late July, and the variety is an excellent pollinator for other varieties. It is rather prone to fruit splitting so is best grown under cover or in lower rainfall regions. The variety is self-fertile.

Summer Sun

The flavour of the fruits of Summer Sun is very good, and it will crop in conditions where other varieties fail.

This variety is partially self-fertile but will crop much better with the assistance of another pollinator such as Celeste, Lapins Cherokee, Stella, Sunburst or Waterloo. The fruits ripen in mid-July.

Sunburst

Sunburst is a self-fertile variety producing a heavy crop of dark red fruits in mid-July.

Sweetheart

Sweetheart is a self-fertile variety that comes into bearing very early in its life (precocious). It is late cropping, its red fruits ripening in late August. The fruits do not ripen all at once, so picking can continue over an extended period.

Sylvia

Sylvia is an early variety that ripens in mid-June. It has a naturally dwarf habit and is self-fertile, making it an excellent choice for small gardens. The large leaves tend to protect the fruit from rainfall, so it resists fruit split. The dark red fruits are sweet and juicy and delightful to eat.

Van

Van is a true black cherry with excellent flavour, and can be eaten fresh or used for cookery. This variety has been used as a parent for many modern varieties. It needs a pollinator such as Celeste, Lapins Cherokee, Stella, Sunburst or Waterloo.

Waterloo

This variety fruited in 1815, the year of the battle of Waterloo. The dark red fruits are juicy and sweet, and it is one of the few heritage varieties of sweet cherry that is self-fertile. Although no pollinator is necessary, it may be tempting to pair it with Napoleon Biggareau

Rootstocks

The development of dwarfing rootstocks has made cherry cultivation easier for both amateur and professional growers by limiting the growth of trees so that they can fit into confined spaces or be grown under cover. It is important to bear in mind that the natural vigour of the scion variety has a strong influence on the ultimate height of the tree as well as the rootstock.

Gisela 5 (Very Dwarfing)

Gisela 5 is a popular rootstock for both commercial and amateur use, and trees usually achieve 3m (10ft) in height. As with all very dwarfing rootstocks, soil conditions must be very good and permanent staking is required. Attention must be paid to watering and nutrition, and the base of the tree must be kept weed-free, preferably by mulching. Trees on this rootstock are suitable for growing in containers. The cherry rootstock 'Tabel' has similar characteristics.

Weigi 2 (Very Dwarfing)

The Weigi 2 rootstock produces trees of a comparable size to those on Gisela 5 but has the advantage of potentially higher fruit yields and fruit size. Trees on this rootstock are suitable for growing in containers.

Gisela 6 (Dwarfing)

Gisela 6 is a more vigorous rootstock than Gisela 5, with bush trees growing to approximately 4.5m (15ft) in height. It is better than Gisela 5 for coping with poorer soils. Trees will need support for three years following planting.

Colt (Intermediate)

Colt is a popular rootstock for community orchards and in situations where a larger tree is required. Trees will often grow to 4.5m (15ft) in height with this rootstock. Trees will need support for three years following planting.

F12.1 (Vigorous)

F12.1 is a rootstock that has been replaced by the more dwarfing kinds for fruit production and is used mainly for ornamental flowering cherries. Sweet cherry varieties on this rootstock are capable of growing to about 6m (20ft) in height, making pruning and harvesting difficult and hazardous.

Pollination

Many of the modern varieties are self-fertile and these generally make good pollination partners for varieties that are not. The pollination of heritage varieties is more complicated as there are many instances of incompatibility between varieties flowering at the same time. Cherries are an early-flowering fruit, so the blossom is susceptible to spring frost damage. Trees grown on the Gisela 5 rootstock can be easily protected from spring frost damage using horticultural fleece, as can the 'Musketeer' range of cherries that are naturally very dwarf.

Diseases, Disorders and Pests

Many pests and diseases of cherries affect other types of top fruit, and their symptoms and control are discussed in previous chapters. These include pear slugworm, spotted wing drosophila, silver leaf and bacterial canker:

Silver leaf and bacterial canker have been discussed in Chapter 5: Growing Plums.

Pear slugworm has been discussed in Chapter 4: Growing Pears.

Spotted wing drosophila has been discussed in Chapter 5: Growing Plums.

Disorders

Fruit Split

Fruit split is usually caused by excessive water entering the fruit via the skin and causing so much internal pressure that the fruit splits. This is different to fruit splits in other fruits, which usually occur when there is heavy rainfall after a period of drought. Some varieties are very resistant to fruit splitting, such as Kordia and Sylvia, whereas others such as Stella are rather prone to it. Fruit splitting due to water entering the fruits via their skins is one of the main reasons why many professional growers grow their trees under polythene covers in tunnels.

Fruit Drop

Fruit drop is a natural occurrence with sweet cherries, and the tree will abort fruitlets that it does not have the resources to develop to maturity. In some years the fruit drop can be excessive and may result in the loss of almost the entire crop. The causes and remedy for fruit drop in cherries are the subject of ongoing research, but initial findings suggest that poor weather at blossom time, including low light levels and temperatures, may be contributory factors. Similarly, poor weather in autumn may result in photosynthetic activity being reduced and lowering the availability of nutrients to sustain fruit development. Pruning the canopy to allow light to enter may assist, and the use of light-coloured or reflective mulches such as white plastic sheet may have the same effect.

Pests

Cherry Black Fly

Cherry black fly is a common aphid (*Myzus carasi*) that appears in dense colonies on young shoots. The populations can build up quickly by the process of asexual reproduction known as parthenogenesis. The aphids secrete a toxin in their saliva causing the leaves to distort, and abort unused sugar causing sticky secretions on lower foliage. The secretions are consumed by fungi, leading to black 'sooty moulds'. On young trees that are establishing the aphid can have a weakening effect; it can be controlled by applications of a contact insecticide based on plant oils or fatty acids that are environmentally benign. On established trees, the time and money spent trying to control this pest is seldom worth it, as the damage caused by the pest is not enough to have a significant effect on cropping. Natural predation by ladybirds, hoverflies and other creatures usually provides sufficient control.

Cherry blackfly is usually only a problem on young trees that are establishing. For older trees, natural predators such as hoverflies and ladybirds usually provide adequate control.

An adult cherry blackfly with some younger nymphs. Like most aphids, this pest multiplies very quickly in favourable conditions.

Pruning and Training

Bush Trees

Sweet cherries grown as bush trees need little pruning once the basic framework has been established.

If pruning a maiden tree, three or four well-spaced branches are selected. Formative pruning is best carried out in spring to promote growth. As the cuts will be small, the likelihood of silver leaf infection is reduced. The selected shoots should be vigorous and healthy as these will form the framework branches of the tree. The central leader is pruned back above the uppermost branch. Any shoots coming from the main trunk are removed. The main framework shoots are reduced by about two-thirds. The trunk should be about 70cm (30in) in length for a tree on Colt and Gisela 6 rootstock, and about 60cm (24in) for trees on Gisela 5 and Weigi 2 rootstocks. For trees on F12.1, grown as a 'half-standard', the main stem should be about 1.5m (5ft) in length.

In the following spring, strong side growths arising from the main framework shoots can be shortened by about a half. Cuts should be made to an outward-facing bud to promote an open goblet shape for the tree. Any weak growths should be removed as well as any growths arising from the trunk below the framework shoots.

In subsequent years, pruning aims to maintain the open shape of the tree. Weak, rubbing and crossing branches should be removed cleanly without leaving a 'stub'. In year four, the timing of the pruning should change from spring to mid-July to minimise silver leaf and bacterial canker infection. Pruning equipment such as saws and secateurs should be sterilised frequently, and certainly when moving from one tree to another.

The formative pruning of bush trees of acid cherries is similar to that of sweet cherries, but from the third year onwards, a quarter of the fruited shoots are removed in favour of a lower-growing replacement shoot. The reason for this difference is that acid cherries fruit on younger wood and this pruning method encourages productive new growth.

Fan-Trained Trees

Cherries are excellent subjects for fan training, and the acid cherry Morello can be grown against a north-facing wall. Sweet cherries need as much sunlight as possible and should be grown against a south- or west-facing wall. Morello and other varieties with low vigour are best grown on a Colt rootstock for fan training; more vigorous varieties would fare better on a Gisela 5, Tabel or Weigi 2 rootstock.

The formative pruning of a fan-trained cherry is exactly the same as for fan-trained apples, as described in Chapter 3: Growing Apples, but the initial pruning cuts are made in spring rather than winter.

Acid cherries grown as fans need slightly different treatment when established. New shoots arising from the main branch framework are thinned out in late July so that they are 5 to 10cm (2 to 4in) apart. These are then tied into supports. At the same time, new shoots coming outwards from the main branches are shortened back to two leaves to keep the tree flat. In late August, the current season's growth is tied into the wire support. This growth will bear next year's fruits. Fruited wood is removed and cut back to a side shoot, which can replace the removed growth.

Thinning

Cherries seldom require thinning as the naturally occurring fruit drop in late spring is usually sufficient to remove excess fruit. Light removal of some fruits from the clusters may be necessary if the fruit set is excessive and the fruit drop light. Thinning should aim to reduce the number of fruits per cluster to about ten. This should be done when the fruitlets are no more than 5mm in diameter.

Watering and Feeding

Trees are best planted in autumn when the combination of residual soil warmth from the summer and adequate soil moisture promotes root development. For the growing season following planting, watering is essential during dry periods to promote vigorous growth. A thorough watering every few days is better than a daily sprinkling to encourage strong root development. A mulch of well-rotted farmyard manure around the base of the tree will help to conserve soil moisture as well as providing essential plant nutrients. If a white plastic mulch is used to maximise light levels, a granular balanced feed containing all the major plant nutrients should be applied in spring before the plastic mulch is put down.

Harvesting and Storage

Cherries should be picked holding the stalks, which should come free from the tree. Detaching the stalk from the cherry will cause a wound that will result in rapid deterioration of the fruit. Harvesting is best carried out on a dry day, and special care must be taken not to damage the delicate fruit. Sweet cherries should be eaten as fresh as possible; they may be stored in the fridge for about four or five days. Both sweet and sour cherries can be frozen or bottled in preserving jars. Both methods require the fruits to be pitted. Pitting a large bowl of cherries can test the patience of a saint, and an inexpensive pitting tool can mercifully speed up the process.

Fan-trained cherries grown in cages. Although expensive, these cages provide excellent protection from birds.

CHAPTER 7

GROWING STRAWBERRIES

According to a survey commissioned by the British Government, strawberries are the most popular fruit with the public, and this is probably not a surprise. Strawberries have a strong association with British summers, picnics and Wimbledon. The person credited with the first serving of strawberries and cream was Cardinal Wolsey, who offered this dessert to impress his guests at Hampton Court Palace in the early sixteenth century. Strawberries may possibly have helped to play their part in the downfall of King Richard III, who may have suffered from an allergy to the fruit: after consuming a bowlful he thought he was being poisoned, and demanded the summary execution of Lord Hastings. A very small percentage of the population can suffer from a strawberry allergy, and can suffer some very unpleasant symptoms.

Strawberries were mentioned in writings by the Romans, but as the small wild strawberries were much smaller than the modern types and had little of their appeal, very few praiseworthy comments were written about them.

Strawberries were cultivated in the Middle Ages in Europe partly as a fruit but also for their medicinal qualities. But it was not until the advent of two species of strawberry, one from North America and one from the southern continent, that the humble strawberry became an opulent delicacy revered the world over.

The movement of cultivated fruits between the old and new worlds was not a one-way passage. In the seventeenth century, the Virginian strawberry, *Fragaria virginiana*, was imported into Britain from North America. The North American strawberry was seen to be an improvement on the native wild strawberry, *Fragaria vesca*, and gardeners started to cultivate it.

In the next century, the Chilean strawberry *Fragaria chiloensis* came to Europe allegedly from a French spy

The small fruits of alpine strawberries have a rich taste, and the plants make an excellent ground cover.

Tabletop strawberries being grown on a commercial holding. This system makes harvesting quicker and more efficient.

A pink-flowered strawberry makes a good subject for the border as well as being a source of tasty fruit.

working in Chile. In a garden in Brittany, the Virginian and the Chilean strawberries hybridised, and the result was 'Fragaria × ananassa' – the modern strawberry. Fragaria × ananassa was named after its pineapple-like flavour. British horticulturists developed varieties of this new hybrid fruit, with further development being carried out all over the world. World production of strawberries is currently over nine million tonnes, and the largest producer is China, followed by the United States. The United Kingdom produces about 150,000 tonnes of strawberries annually, with increasing amounts being grown on the 'tabletop' system in coir modules under polythene tunnels and glasshouses.

As pleasant as strawberries grown under intensive systems may be, there is little doubt that home-produced fruit has superior flavour. Without the need to generate profit, the home gardener can choose the variety and cultivation and storage method that will give the most flavoursome fruit. The variety influences flavour, and some of the heritage varieties such as Royal Sovereign and Cambridge Favourite are considered two of the best in this respect. Commercial varieties may be selected for colour and shape uniformity, and ease of picking and storage life are more important than flavour.

Many consider that the medium in which the strawberries are grown will influence flavour, with the tastiest fruit from plants grown in soil rather than a growing medium. The irrigation of the plants will also influence flavour, and plants supplied with copious amounts of water by automatic irrigation systems can lack the intensity of flavour of plants grown with less water. Lastly, strawberries that have been chilled after harvest seldom have the same flavour as those that have been kept at field temperature.

Growing strawberries is not without its challenges, despite the obvious benefits of superior flavour. Strawberries attract many pests and diseases and need careful cultivation for best results.

As with many fruits, strawberries can add ornament to gardens. Perpetual strawberries can be used to grace hanging baskets and containers, and some varieties have attractive pink flowers.

Alpine strawberries (*Fragaria vesca*) make superb ground coverers, suppressing weed with their evergreen foliage and adding ornament with their small white flowers followed by tiny, flavoursome berries. It is difficult to fill a bowl with alpine strawberries on account of their size, but the fruits make a great snack whilst weeding the borders.

Types of Strawberry

There are three main types of outdoor strawberry: summer-fruiting varieties, perpetual strawberries (everbearers) and alpine strawberries.

Summer-Fruiting Strawberries

Summer-fruiting strawberries are the most popular, which have their cropping concentrated into a period of about two or three weeks. This type produces the largest berries and the heaviest crop. Summer-fruiting varieties are available as early, mid-season and late-cropping types. The cropping period for this type is from early to midsummer.

Perpetual Strawberries (Everbearers)

Perpetual strawberries produce fruits in flushes from early summer until the first autumn frosts. The berries are smaller than the summer-flowering types, and the crop is smaller. Their cropping potential is reduced in their second year and so they are best treated as a short-term crop and removed after cropping has finished in autumn.

Alpine Strawberries

Alpine strawberries produce delicious small fruits. They have neat foliage and small attractive flowers, and make an excellent ground cover amongst shrubs. They relish a cool, semi-shaded position, and are relatively trouble-free. They can be raised cheaply from seed.

Purchasing Plants

Strawberries are rather prone to disease, in particular viral diseases, and it is important to start with certified disease-free plants from a reputable supplier. Specialist fruit growers will sell these as a matter of course, and garden centres will source their stock from these specialists. It is important to avoid the temptation to buy or accept runners from amateur growers as these will probably be virus-infected.

Plants can be purchased as plugs in spring. This is a popular method of raising strawberry plants, and plug plants are usually bought by commercial growers for planting in modules (grow bags). As these are mass produced, supermarkets may sell packs of strawberry plants as plugs at a competitive price. Plugs are commonly available from mail-order suppliers.

Larger plants can be bought from garden centres and will establish more quickly than plug plants. Seed-raised alpine strawberries are usually sold as potted plants.

In late summer, mail-order suppliers sell strawberry runners. Runners are horizontal stems that grow along the ground producing plantlets at intervals. The plantlets root and can be detached from the mother plant. Strawberry runners are usually trimmed before despatch to minimise water loss. They need to be planted in prepared soil as soon as they are received.

Some specialist suppliers offer 'cold-stored' runners. These have been chilled to enable flowering and fruiting within 60 days from planting.

Selected Varieties

There are numerous strawberry varieties, and every year new ones are offered by the nursery trade; each new introduction is lauded with superlatives, such as 'outstanding' and 'excellent flavour'. The following is a list of noteworthy varieties.

Alexandria

Alexandria is a popular alpine variety that produces comparatively large fruits with the intensely aromatic flavour of wild strawberries. It is easily available from seed suppliers.

Alice

Alice is an early summer-fruiting variety developed by the East Malling Research Station in Kent. It produces masses of regular conical berries that are sweet and juicy. Disease resistance is good.

Baron von Solemacher

Baron von Solemacher is an alpine strawberry from Germany that is similar to Alexandria, with fruits of a similar size and eating quality. Like Alexandria, it is available from many seed suppliers.

Bolero

Bolero is an everbearer that crops reliably from mid-August to the first frosts. Fruit quality is very good, as is its disease resistance.

Calypso

Calypso is a popular everbearer variety that produces good crops of large, regular-shaped berries. Fruiting starts in mid-July, but the main cropping months are August and September. The flavour is good, and this variety shows resistance to verticillium wilt.

Cambridge Favourite

Cambridge Favourite is an established variety that is still offered by many nurseries. The strongly flavoured berries hold their shape well, and are ready from mid-June onwards. For an older variety it is surprisingly disease-resistant.

Elsanta

Elsanta is a popular variety with both amateur and professional growers. The orange-red berries are delicious, and the variety is quite adaptable, growing on a range of soils. The berries start to ripen in mid-June and continue to mid-July.

Flamenco

Flamenco is a heavy-cropping everbearer variety with large, bright red, conical fruits. Cropping starts in July and runs to October, with the main period in September. This variety has good verticillium resistance.

Florence

Florence is a reliable and good late-cropper, with dark red, sweet berries that will last well. Mildew resistance is good.

Hapil

Hapil is a mid-season variety with heavy crops of sweet-flavoured berries.

Honeoye

Honeoye is an early-cropping variety with large, bright red berries. This variety is susceptible to mildew but its merits outweigh this drawback.

Korona

This early variety is very heavy-cropping, and the berries are soft and juicy, making them ideal for sauces.

Malling Opal

Malling Opal has become a deservedly popular everbearing variety, with the fruits ripening from early August onwards and continuing right up until the first frosts. If brought under protection, the plants will continue cropping until much later. The sweet fruits are rather soft, and the variety has some resistance to powdery mildew.

Mara de Bois

Mara de Bois is sometimes classed as an everbearer or an alpine type. The fruits are the size of everbearing strawberries but have the aromatic qualities and flavour intensity of alpine strawberries. This variety is widely grown in France and is popular with chefs.

Pegasus

Pegasus is a late summer-fruiting variety with sweet, juicy berries and good disease resistance.

Royal Sovereign

Royal Sovereign is a variety for the strawberry enthusiast who is prepared to make minor sacrifices to get the best-tasting fruit. This mid-season heritage variety is neither heavy-cropping nor disease-resistant, but the fruit is exquisitely flavoured.

Sonata

Sonata is a mid-season variety, and the well-flavoured berries have a good balance of sweetness and acidity. It also withstands the vagaries of the British weather, coping with both hot and wet conditions.

Symphony

Symphony is an excellent late variety for northern and western areas, as it copes with damper conditions. The tasty fruits are medium to large.

Vibrant

Vibrant is an early summer-fruiting variety. The flowers on each truss are limited so the fruit tends to be large. It may produce a second, smaller crop of berries in September if the summer temperatures are not too hot. The berries are bright red.

Pollination

Botanists classify the sweet berries of strawberries as a false fruit because strictly speaking, the actual fruits of a strawberry are what we consider to be the seeds on the outside of the berry. The edible strawberry is a swollen flower receptacle that carries many fruits. To get evenly shaped and reasonably large berries, pollinating insects must make several visits to the flower. According to research in Australia, between six to fifteen pollination visits are required to fertilise a strawberry flower fully. Strawberries can be wind pollinated but this is of minor significance when compared with insect pollination. Poorly pollinated flowers result in small and misshapen berries.

Some early strawberry varieties are prone to having flowers destroyed by late spring frosts, and monitoring weather forecasts that warn of spring frosts is a good idea when growing early strawberries. Covering the plants with horticultural fleece at night will provide frost protection, but it must be removed during the daytime to allow pollinating insects access to the flowers.

Most strawberry varieties are self-fertile and do not need another pollinating variety. All the strawberry varieties listed previously are self-fertile.

Planting and Aftercare

Strawberries appreciate a sunny spot, except for alpine types that relish semi-shade. It is important to remove all perennial weeds before planting as weed control is difficult in a strawberry bed. Strawberry beds need to be rotated regularly as the soil will rapidly build up pests and pathogens, and so a new planting should not be positioned where an older planting has been removed. Summer strawberries should be replanted every three to four years, and everbearers are removed after they have finished their first crop.

Strawberries prefer a mildly acid soil (pH 6.0 to 6.5) that has been enriched by digging in organic material such as rotted manure or garden compost. A base dressing of a compound fertiliser such as Growmore or blood, fish and bone will help to get the plants off to a good start. The ground should not have been used for a crop of chrysanthemums, potatoes or tomatoes as these can all carry the fungal disease verticillium wilt that affects strawberries. Strawberries should not be planted in grow bags that have had a previous crop of tomatoes.

Small plug plants are best potted into 9cm (3.5in) pots and grown on before planting out. Potted plants are suitable for immediate planting into soil or containers.

Strawberry runners need planting on immediate receipt, so it is vital that the soil is prepared beforehand. Dig a hole into the prepared soil using a trowel that is large enough to accommodate the roots; excessively long roots can be lightly trimmed back. Plant the runners so that the junction of the basal leaves and root system is at soil level. Firm the soil lightly, and water in the plants. The runners will need to be kept watered until they are established.

Strawberries are often grown in containers. In the United Kingdom most commercial strawberry growers use modules (grow bags) as this prevents the

A straw mulch protects strawberry fruits from damage.

build-up of soil-borne diseases that can have a serious effect on the crop. Commercial modules usually have coir as the main ingredient, as this material can be sterilised and reused. Amateur growers can use grow bags commonly sold in garden centres. The cheaper types of grow bag have a limited amount of growing medium and are too thin to manage the water content in them; the thicker premium types are a better choice. Some suppliers offer refillable grow bags that can help to minimise plastic waste. As strawberries are often a short-term crop, ordinary multipurpose compost will suffice. Depending on the size of the grow bag, between three and five plants are inserted in each bag.

Deep and wide troughs make excellent containers for strawberry growing, but decorative strawberry pots are difficult to manage in terms of keeping each plant sufficiently watered.

Strawberry beds are planted with the plants 35 to 40cm (14 to 16in) apart in rows. Sometimes the plants are grown through a polythene sheet to act as a weed suppressant and to keep the fruit off the soil to minimise rotting. The best polythene to use has a white upper surface to reflect light and a black lower surface. Carefully cut compost bags can make a suitable substitute and good use of plastic that might otherwise go to waste.

The alternative to using a plastic mulch is straw, but this should not have been treated with hormone-type weedkillers, which are persistent and can harm the crop. The straw is applied as a generous layer between the plants, but it must not be applied too early to avoid frost damage. This is because on frosty nights in late spring, the straw prevents the soil from mitigating the effects of frost by releasing its warmth accumulated during the day. For early summer crops, the mulch should be applied as the fruits are beginning to set.

If everbearing varieties are planted whilst in flower, the flowers should be removed to allow the plants to establish first. Summer-fruiting and alpine strawberries can be planted whilst in flower as this will not adversely affect cropping.

Propagation

Most strawberries propagate themselves with ease by means of runners, but taking runners from established beds runs the very great risk of spreading viruses as well as other diseases. Viral diseases are difficult to detect, but their transmission via aphids, nematodes and the transport of infected material is inevitable. It may be worth the risk of allowing runners still attached to the parent plant to root in pots of compost, and then detaching them afterwards to establish as new plants, but this is very much open to debate. Commercial growers always use certified disease-free plants from specialist growers as they are not prepared to take a risk with their crops, and amateur growers should be equally wary.

Seed-raised plants will be generally virus-free on germination as the virus is unable to enter the seed embryo via the mother plant. Although available from seed suppliers, large-fruited strawberries raised from seed are seldom satisfactory.

Alpine strawberries can be raised easily and cheaply from seed. Seeds germinate best if chilled in a refrigerator and then sown in a greenhouse or cold frame in spring. High temperatures will inhibit germination. After sowing on a suitable compost, the seeds should be covered lightly. Fine vermiculite is ideal for this purpose.

Once the seedlings have developed two true leaves, they should be pricked out and potted into 9cm (3.5in) pots to grow on before planting out. Alpine strawberries will readily seed themselves and these seedlings can be transplanted if required.

Management of Strawberry Plants

Everbearer varieties are best removed after their first period of cropping as they seldom perform well in their second year. Summer-fruiting varieties can be retained for up to four years before a combination of soil-borne diseases and viruses starts to limit crop production.

Alpine strawberries can remain indefinitely. The foliage of summer-fruiting varieties should be sheared off after fruiting to remove foliage diseases such as powdery mildew. Unless used for propagation, strawberry runners should be removed as they appear.

The soil or medium in which strawberry plants are growing must be kept moist but should not be waterlogged as this can cause fungal diseases. Strawberries appreciate a high-potassium liquid feed applied at fortnightly intervals from the onset of flowering until fruiting has finished. Liquid tomato food is ideal for this purpose.

Diseases, Disorders and Pests

Diseases

Unfortunately strawberries are affected by many diseases and are eaten by several pests. Keeping the plants pest- and disease-free requires vigilance, but is well worth the effort.

Botrytis (Grey Mould)

Botrytis is a common fungal disease that attacks both ornamental and edible plants. It is usually first noticed on fruits that turn soft and brown, and then become covered by a grey fungal deposit. There is no approved fungicide available to amateur growers, and the best control is good cultivation and hygiene. Any affected fruits and growth should be removed immediately, and the use of nitrogen-rich fertilisers minimised to prevent excessive soft growth.

Powdery Mildew

Strawberry mildew is a common fungal disease that reduces cropping by weakening the plant. The foliage looks as if it has been dusted with talcum powder. It can be controlled by plant-oil-based mildewcides, as well as ensuring better watering and adequate plant spacing.

Red Core

Red core is a serious soil-borne disease caused by a fungus-like organism. The pathogen *Phytophthora fragariae* is a close relative of the one that causes potato blight. When cut open, the thicker roots show a red discolouration. The plants become stunted and unproductive and may die. The disease is associated with soils prone to waterlogging. On heavy clay soils

Strawberry mildew is a troublesome fungal disease of strawberries.

Red core of strawberries is a serious disease caused by a fungus-like organism.

it is advisable to plant the rows in ridges, or plant in containers to minimise the threat of this disease. The pathogen is very persistent in the soil, and following the removal of an infected strawberry bed, the ground should not be used to grow strawberries for five years. There is no chemical control available for red core.

Verticillium Wilt

Verticillium wilt is another serious soil-borne disease and is one of the main reasons why commercial strawberry growers use coir modules rather than soil for growing their plants. The disease is caused by two soil-borne fungal species, *Verticillium dahliae* and *V. albo-atrum*. The fungi enter the plant via the root stem, and symptoms start on the outer leaves first with these starting to wilt. The disease moves to the whole plant, which usually wilts and dies. The plant may recover temporarily in cooler, wetter weather but usually this is a lost cause. The fungi are very persistent in the soil and if the bed is infected, replanting with strawberries should not occur within fifteen years. Use coir modules for future crops. No chemical control is available to amateur growers.

Disorders

Phyllody

Phyllody is a plant disorder in which parts of the flower are replaced by leafy structures. Strawberries are commonly affected. These misshapen fruits sprout leaves and are inedible. There are two main causes of phyllody in strawberries: one is environmental, and the second is a mycoplasma infection. Frost damage to the flowers and moisture stress are the two main environmental factors, and the effects are usually short-lived. Once the environmental triggers are gone, the disorder goes away, and normal flowers are produced. Mycoplasmas are pathogenic bacteria that cannot be treated and cause permanent damage. The only remedy is to destroy affected plants.

Black Eye

Black eye is caused by frost damage to the flowers, and the centre of the flower turns black. The flower is effectively destroyed and cannot produce a fruit. The remedy is the use of horticultural fleece as frost protection. Mulching the plants too early with straw can also increase the possibility of frost damage, as it prevents the soil releasing its warmth during cold nights.

Pests

Slugs and Snails

It would be unreasonable to expect slugs and snails to leave our delicious strawberries alone. Conveniently located at ground level, strawberries are a sitting target for molluscs. Until recently, gardeners would use pellets containing the active ingredient metaldehyde, which is harmful to pets and wildlife. Metaldehyde is now thankfully banned for home gardeners and has been replaced by ferric phosphate, which is less harmful, but not entirely harmless. Ferric phosphate affects the calcium metabolism in the gut system of slugs and snails, rendering them incapable of eating; they die within three to six days. Ferric phosphate can affect earthworms.

Slugs and snails are more abundant in wet weather, and their slime trails are a clear indication of their presence. Buried yoghurt pots or jars partly filled with water or beer can reduce numbers by catching and drowning the hapless molluscs.

Using nematodes is becoming an increasingly popular non-chemical method of mollusc control, but the instructions from the suppliers must be followed carefully. Attention needs to be paid to the soil temperature and moisture, and the nematodes are best applied in the evening as they can be damaged by ultraviolet light. An application of nematodes usually lasts for about six weeks before a repeat application may be necessary. There are many species of nematode: some are predatory and parasitic on a range of pests, others are a serious pest of plants including strawberry, and also a vector for viruses.

Encouraging natural predators such as amphibians and hedgehogs helps in the war against molluscs, though birds are both friends and foes as they may turn their attention to the juicy berries.

Strawberry Aphid

The strawberry aphid *Chaetosiphon fragaefolii* does little direct damage, but it is an important vector for many viruses. Natural plant oils and fatty acid-based insecticides can give reasonable control, but they have short persistence so repeat applications are necessary.

Strawberry Seed Beetle

This small black beetle is very common, but its damage is often mistaken for that caused by slugs. Strawberry seed beetle is common in dry weather, and it favours sandy soils. The small black beetles feed on the flesh as well as the seeds of strawberries, and the damage is usually seen on the underside of the fruit. The beetle feeds on a variety of plants including many common weeds. Control of the beetles is difficult, but keeping the strawberry bed free of weeds and debris will help.

Vine Weevil

This black nocturnal beetle with its characteristic snout is a common pest of many garden plants. The adults (all female) are active after pupating in spring. By night the adult females feed on a wide range of host plants

Vine-weevil larvae. These troublesome pests eat the root system of a wide variety of plants, including strawberry.

Adult vine weevils usually leave a notch on the leaf margin of a host plant.

such as hydrangea and bergenia, and lay their eggs at the base of suitable host plants, including strawberry. The eggs hatch in summer and the larvae begin feeding on the roots of the host plant. The symptoms of vine-weevil attack include stunted growth and wilting, even when the soil is moist. In cases of heavy infestations, it is possible to detach the foliage from the remains of the root system. The creamy white, plump larvae with a brown head are easy to spot amongst the roots of host plants.

There are several methods to control vine weevil, and some can be used in combination to increase effectiveness. Nematodes are now popular with gardeners. These are a different species to that used for mollusc control. As with all nematode control methods, it is important to take account of soil moisture and temperature and the presence of the pest. Usually, nematodes for vine-weevil control are applied in late summer when the eggs have hatched into larvae and the soil temperature is high enough for the nematodes to be feeding.

Leaving small pots full of straw around feeding sites for adults can act as useful traps; these are emptied out during the day and the weevils destroyed. Care must be taken not to kill useful predators such as the violet beetle, which plays a vital role in pest control.

Spraying plants that the adults are feeding on can reduce populations of vine weevil. Many garden insecticides are not suitable for use on edibles, but can be used on ornamental plants that are food for adult vine weevils.

Sometimes a plant can be used as bait for vine-weevil larvae. The herbaceous perennial heuchera is greatly favoured by vine weevils and is easily and cheaply raised from seed. Growing a bed of heuchera will make an excellent bait. The plants can be dug up in late summer and the roots carefully examined for vine-weevil larvae and the pests destroyed. Leaving the larvae on the bird table will make a treat for robins.

Encouraging natural predators such as ground beetles will also prove beneficial in controlling vine weevils.

Heucheras can be used to attract vine weevil as a sacrificial plant.

Birds

Birds will make a determined effort to eat strawberries, and netting is the best deterrent. Decoys and scarers such as hawk kites and suspended compact discs can work for a limited amount of time before the birds become used to them.

Spotted Wing Drosophila

Spotted wing drosophila is native to Asia and was introduced to the USA by accident in 2010. Since then it has become established in Europe, including the UK. The damage caused by this pest has been discussed in Chapter 5: Growing Plums.

Watering and Feeding

Strawberries resent waterlogging, but water is required to swell the developing fruits. The soil or growing medium needs to be kept evenly moist by diligent watering during dry periods. Strawberries need fertilisers that are rich in potassium. A solid fertiliser can be applied to the soil surface at the recommended rate, and supplemented by a high-potassium liquid feed when the plants come into flower.

Harvesting and Storage

Strawberries are harvested when the fruits have developed their full colouration and are soft and aromatic by severing the fruit stalk using a fingernail or snips. For the best possible flavour the fruits should be harvested immediately before use, as chilled fruits seldom taste as good as those kept at room temperature. The fruits can be kept in a refrigerator for about five days if absolutely necessary. Excess fruit can be made into delicious conserves or sauces.

CHAPTER 8

GROWING CANE FRUITS

Cane fruits include raspberries, blackberries and their numerous hybrids: they all belong to the plant genus *Rubus* and are members of the rose family. The natural distribution of the genus *Rubus* is extensive throughout the globe, covering large areas of North America, Europe and Asia. Both raspberries and blackberries have been foraged for millennia for both their nutritional and medicinal properties. The Romans cultivated raspberries throughout their empire, and King Edward I encouraged the cultivation of the fruit in England.

Raspberries are valued for their exquisite flavour but are also rich in vitamins and antioxidants. Raspberry leaves were valued for making medicinal teas, and the juice of the fruits for making dyes and inks.

Picking wild blackberries in Britain is a pleasant pastime in late summer, provided that the pain from scratches and wasp stings is outweighed by the benefits of the fruit. Many cultivated blackberry varieties are mercifully thorn-free and produce larger berries than their wild counterparts.

Cane fruits are favoured by pollinators and are particularly popular with bees.

Most blackberry and raspberry varieties flower and fruit on canes that have grown the previous year, and these are called 'floricane' varieties. Some varieties of cane fruit flower and fruit on the current season's growth, and these are called 'primocane' varieties.

These fruits are self-fertile and do not need a pollinator.

Raspberries

Raspberries are the most popular cane fruit and give a very good rate of return in terms of quantity of fruit per square metre. There are two main types of raspberry: summer-fruiting varieties are floricane types and will fruit on one-year-old canes, while autumn-fruiting raspberries are primocane types and fruit on the current season's growth. It is possible to obtain a moderate crop the following summer from autumn raspberries by leaving the canes unpruned after fruiting. The fruit flourishes in moderately acidic soils ideally in full sun, but will tolerate light shade.

Raspberries are best purchased in the autumn as bare-rooted plants, usually bundled in packs of five or ten canes; these usually work out cheaper than buying individually potted canes in summer. Between late autumn and early winter is the best time to establish raspberry canes. It is important to buy certified virus-free stock from reputable suppliers as raspberries are prone to viral infection that can have a detrimental effect on cropping.

Raspberry Tulameen – this new long-caned variety produces heavy crops of large, sweet berries with an excellent flavour in mid-summer.

Raspberry Golden Everest – a reliable, yellow-fruited variety.

Raspberry Glen Clova – valued for its long cropping period.

Raspberry Autumn Bliss – this is considered to be one of the finest-tasting autumn raspberries. The berries are picked between August and October; they have a firm texture and sweet taste.

Selected Summer-Fruiting Varieties

Glen Ample

Glen Ample is a very popular mid-season variety that has a long cropping period and produces heavy yields of fruit. This variety has good disease resistance.

Glen Clova

Glen Clova is a very popular early-to-mid-season variety cropping over a comparatively long period, which is particularly useful if you only have space for one variety. The firm fruits freeze well.

Golden Everest

Golden Everest is the original yellow-fruited variety. The fruits are deliciously sweet and freeze well. Cropping is reliable.

Malling Admiral

Malling Admiral is another popular variety that produces vigorous canes. The fruits are medium to large with a deep red colour, and are harvested from late July to mid-August. Disease resistance is good.

Malling Jewell

Malling Jewell is a deservedly popular variety that has compact growth, and the deep red flavoursome berries retain their firmness for at least a week after picking.

Ruby Beauty

Ruby Beauty is a novelty primocane variety with dwarf canes that grow to approximately 1m (3ft) in height. It is sold as a 'patio' variety for growing in containers. Cropping is moderate.

Tulameen

Tulameen is a late-season variety producing wonderfully sweet red berries over a long period. The canes are vigorous and free from prickles. The berries retain their firmness for a reasonable time after picking.

Selected Autumn-Fruiting Varieties

All Gold

This variety has particularly sweet yellow berries from mid-August to mid-October. The berries have a slight tendency to crumble, but this is more than offset by the outstanding flavour.

Autumn Bliss

Autumn Bliss is a reliable red-berried variety that crops from August to October and has good disease resistance.

Joan J

Joan J is a red-fruited variety with a long cropping period that starts in July and finishes in October. Cropping is particularly heavy, but tends to tail off in the second half of the cropping period. The large berries have a superb flavour, and the canes are free of prickles.

Polka

Polka is a new red-fruited variety from Poland and has rapidly gained popularity on account of its heavy cropping and its extended cropping period, which starts in July and extends to the first frosts. Flavour and disease resistance are good, and the canes are virtually prickle-free.

Planting and Training

Raspberries like a moist, slightly acidic soil that has been generously supplied with organic material. A word of caution is necessary, as some organic materials, such as mushroom compost, can make the soil too alkaline for raspberries. Garden compost and farmyard manure can also be alkaline, but this can be corrected using sulphur chips to acidify the soil. In heavy or wet soils, planting the canes on 8cm (3in) ridges will reduce the possibility of waterlogging that can cause serious fungal diseases such as phytophthora root rot.

In most instances, a support system for raspberries needs to be installed before planting the canes. A simple system is to use a single fence system. This

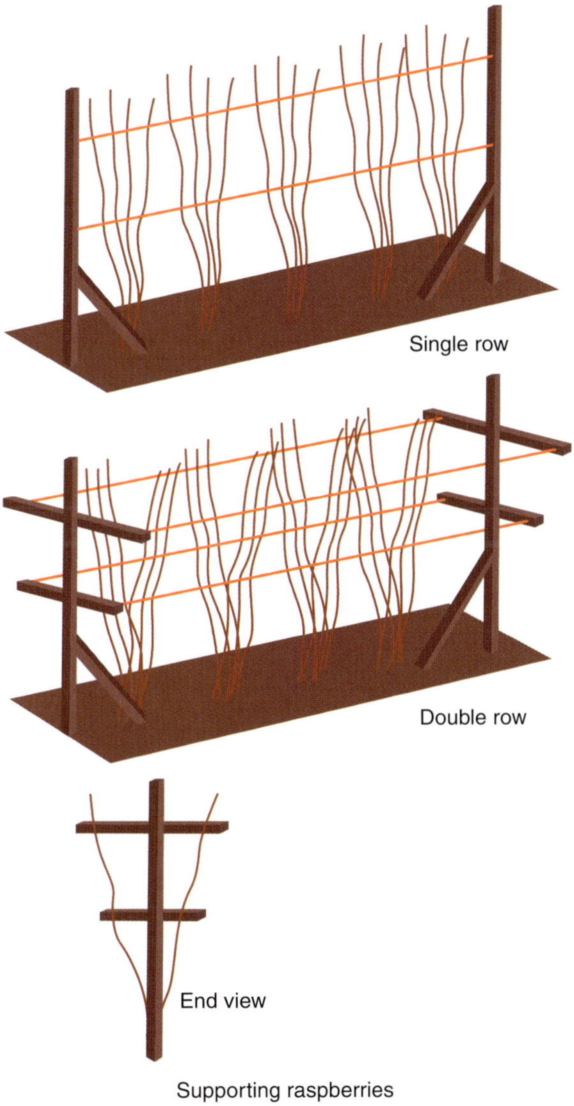

Supporting raspberries using a post-and-wire system.

consists of 7.5cm (3in) square or rounded fence posts and strong fencing wire similar to the support system used for cordon fruit trees. The posts should be 1.8m (6ft) tall and inserted into the ground to a depth of 75cm (30in). The end posts are braced, and if necessary, intermediate posts are placed 3.6m (11.8ft) apart. Horizontal wires are positioned and tensioned at 60cm (24in) intervals. The canes are tied to the wire support using soft twine.

A variant of the single fence system is to use the parallel wires system. The posts are inserted exactly the same way as for the single fence, but two short lengths of wood are attached to each post, one at the top and one approximately 60cm (24in) from the ground. Strong wire is attached to the ends of these pieces of timber so that the canes can be trained between them. Cross-supports of thin wire or jute are then fixed at 60cm spacings at right angles to the strong wire so that canes are adequately supported without tying. The parallel wires system promotes heavier cropping than the single fence.

It is possible to grow two or three plants against a single 7.5cm (3in) post if space is restricted. Raspberries can also be grown in containers using bamboo canes for support. A loam-based growing medium such as John Innes Number 3 is ideal for raspberries.

All perennial weeds must be eradicated before planting raspberry canes to prevent a serious maintenance

Summer-fruiting raspberry canes in winter. These are usually pruned back lightly in February.

A neglected raspberry bed. This is likely to be virus-infected and should be dug up and a different crop grown in its place.

problem. Perennial weeds growing amongst the dense, fibrous roots of raspberries are very difficult to control effectively.

Raspberry canes are planted at 45 to 60cm (18 to 24in) spacings and given a 7cm (3in) thick mulch of garden compost or a similar organic material immediately after planting. Autumn- and summer-fruiting raspberries should be cut down to about 25cm (10in) immediately after planting if dormant, but the young canes of container-grown summer-fruiting varieties should be left unpruned as these will bear fruit next year.

The pruning of raspberries is simple, as summer-fruiting varieties with few exceptions are floricane types and fruit on growth made in the previous season. After fruiting the canes are cut out to ground level. The current season's growth of summer-fruiting raspberries is left unpruned in autumn. Any growth extending over the top wire is bent over and tied in. In February, the canes are untied and cut back to a bud about 10cm (4in) above the top wire.

Raspberries will readily multiply by suckering. Allow only about six to eight canes per plant to prevent overcrowding and maintain fruit quality.

Autumn-fruiting raspberries are primocane types and fruit on the current season's growth. For purely autumn cropping, the canes are cut down to ground level in November. Many autumn-fruiting varieties can produce a moderate crop the following summer if lightly pruned. The stronger canes are selected so that about six per metre row are pruned to about 1m (3ft) in height. After cropping in summer, the canes are cut down to ground level. Autumn-fruiting varieties should be well established for a couple of years before double cropping.

Propagation

Raspberries readily reproduce by suckering, but although this seems to be an easy form of propagation, detaching and replanting these suckers is seldom worthwhile and is fraught with problems. Raspberries are easily and rapidly infected by several viruses that are incurable, and which adversely affect cropping. Taking suckers from plants that are more than one year old is likely to result in virus-infected plants. Although a more expensive option, it is better to buy certified material from virus-free plants from a reputable supplier than to use suckers from established plants.

Diseases, Disorders and Pests

Cane Blight

Cane blight is a serious disease of raspberries caused by the fungus *Leptosphaeria coniothyrium*: it causes the death of canes and a severe reduction in cropping. During the summer, the foliage of affected canes withers and their bases become dark brown and brittle, and snap off early. The fungus gains entry to the canes by means of pruning cuts, frost damage or wounds caused by the cane midge. The disease is most likely to attack weak plants, so sufficient mulching to retain soil moisture, and ensuring the adequate spacing of canes, will help to prevent this disease. Affected canes should be cut off at ground level and the secateurs sterilised between cuts. The canes should be burned or put into green waste for recycling.

Spur Blight

Spur blight is a fungal disease that causes purple patches on the canes and will reduce cropping. Affected canes should be burned or put into green waste for recycling.

Phytophthora Root Rot

Phytophthora is a genus of fungus-like organisms that can cause devastating plant diseases such as potato blight. Phytophthora root rot of raspberries is a serious soil-borne disease that has led to many commercial growers growing their crop in containers that are isolated from the soil. Canes are killed in the first year of growth or sometimes early in the second year. The disease is often associated with waterlogging or poor drainage, and canes planted in heavy soils are best planted on ridges to facilitate drainage in the root zone. In addition, the trench for planting should be double dug. An alternative is to grow the canes in raised beds or containers. There is no chemical control available for phytophthora and the only remedy is the destruction of the affected canes. New canes should not be planted in soil affected by phytophthora. The varieties Malling Admiral, Malling Jewel and Polka show good resistance to phytophthora.

Raspberries in a commercial plantation. The special pots prevent fungal infection from the soil contaminating the crop.

Phytophthora disease is very hard to control.

Viruses

Raspberries are host to numerous viruses that are transmitted by the large and small European raspberry aphids as well as soil-dwelling nematodes. Plant viruses are practically incurable and infect almost every cell in the plant, inevitably having a detrimental effect on growth and cropping. Some are noticeable by their patterning on foliage, such as the mosaic viruses, others have no easily recognisable symptoms (latent viruses). Specialist nurseries can remove viruses from infected plants by a technique known as micro-propagation, in which tiny pieces of plant from the growth points are cultured and then grown on to make new plants. These virus-free plants are then used to make new stock.

Care is taken to exclude aphids from the growing stock, and plants are inspected by a government inspectorate before certifying that they are virus-free. The spread of a virus in a planting of raspberries can be slowed by the control of aphids and not replanting raspberries in the same place after removing a planting. However, even with careful management, raspberries will become infected over time, and it is recommended that plantings are replaced between seven and twelve years in a different position.

A raspberry plant with a viral infection.

Magnesium Deficiency

Magnesium deficiency is characterised by leaf yellowing between the veins (interveinal chlorosis) on older leaves, and it gradually moves to all parts of the plant if not rectified. The deficiency is most common on acid sandy soils that have a low organic matter content but high levels of potassium. Potassium and magnesium ions are mutually antagonistic and so an abundance of potassium will interfere with the uptake of magnesium by the roots. Applying a magnesium-based fertiliser to the soil in either liquid or solid form is unlikely to be effective. Magnesium deficiency is best treated using a foliar spray of a solution of magnesium sulphate (Epsom salts). Approximately 500g (18oz) of magnesium sulphate is dissolved in 10ltr (2.2gal) of water and sprayed on to the foliage to the point of run-off as soon as the signs of the deficiency become apparent; this is repeated two or three times at two-week intervals.

Iron Deficiency

Like magnesium, iron is sometimes deficient in raspberries. However, unlike magnesium, iron deficiency is usually encountered on alkaline rather than acid soils, and the deficiency is usually seen as a yellowing of the younger rather than the older leaves. Ericaceous fertilisers containing chelated iron provide a fast remedy for this deficiency. It is also worth testing the pH of the soil if iron deficiency is encountered, and if it is too high, steps should be taken to acidify the soil.

Raspberry Beetle

Although annoying, this pest is seldom a major problem and can often be tolerated. The larvae of this small brown beetle eat the fruit at the stalk end, resulting in small, greyish-brown dried patches. Occasionally the small brownish-white larvae can be seen feeding inside the fruits. The pest is most active in early summer, and so summer-fruiting varieties are most likely to be affected. The damage on autumn-fruiting varieties is likely to be minimal. Adult females lay their eggs on the stalk end of the developing fruits from May to mid-July, and the larvae hatch and begin feeding on the stalk end of the fruit before moving on to the plug. In late summer the larvae drop to the soil where they pupate.

If deemed necessary, some control of this pest can be achieved by encouraging predators such as birds and ground beetles. A water trap that secretes a host plant odour (karimone) is available from some specialist suppliers, and this will help to control populations of both male and female beetles.

Magnesium deficiency in raspberries is easily dealt with by a foliar application of magnesium sulphate.

Cane Midge

The cane midge (*Resseliella theobaldi*) can be a serious pest of summer raspberries. The larvae of this midge are pink in colour and grow to about 4mm (¼in) in length. Eggs are laid in the cracks in the bark of young canes and so varieties prone to natural cane splitting are most susceptible to the pest. These include Glen Prosen, Malling Admiral and Malling Jewel. The larvae feed beneath the bark and fall to the ground to pupate two or three weeks later. There are usually three generations of this pest, and the third generation overwinters as pupae in the soil before emerging in spring. Symptoms of midge attack include wilting or the failure of foliage to emerge from fruiting canes after winter. If the bark is removed, the feeding sites of this pest will be discoloured.

This is not a pest of autumn raspberries because these are not double-cropped, and the pest is destroyed when the canes are removed after cropping in winter, thus breaking the life cycle.

There is no chemical control available for cane midge to amateur gardeners, but populations can be reduced by lightly cultivating the soil around the base of the canes in winter. Deep cultivation is not recommended as raspberries resent root disturbance.

Large and Small European Raspberry Aphids

Both species of aphid cause little direct damage to raspberries but are vectors of viral diseases that are serious. The large European raspberry aphid, *Amphorophora idaei*, is a yellowish-green aphid growing to about 4mm (¼in) long. The aphid overwinters as eggs at the base of the canes, and in March the eggs hatch and the nymphs move up the canes to feed on the growing tips. In summer, winged adults appear and migrate on to other raspberry plants.

The small European raspberry aphid, *Aphis idaei*, is much smaller than its larger counterpart, growing to about 2mm long. The yellowish aphids can form dense colonies in spring, feeding on actively growing shoots. In winter, the aphid overwinters as eggs on leaf axils and buds towards the top of canes.

Aphids can be controlled by regular spraying with natural plant-oil-based insecticides and the encouragement of natural predators such as ladybirds.

Birds

Birds relish raspberries, and blackbirds are particularly adept at picking and eating them. Deterrents such as scarers and decoy predators may have some effect, but this is usually short term as birds soon realise that they are being duped. Netting is the most effective control method, and the parallel wire system is the easiest to net.

Spotted Wing Drosophila

Spotted wing drosophila is a new pest to the UK but has the potential to be devastating. The symptoms and control of this pest have been discussed in the relevant section in Chapter 5: Growing Plums.

Watering and Feeding

Raspberries like a moist but not waterlogged soil. Mulching with well-rotted manure will help to conserve soil moisture. Additional watering may be necessary during periods of drought in summer. A potassium-rich compound fertiliser applied in early spring will support strong growth and cropping. If cane growth is weak, an additional feed with ammonium sulphate will promote cane growth as well as acidifying the soil.

Harvesting and Storage

Raspberries need regular harvesting, especially in summer. The fruits when ripe will be brightly coloured and plump, and will detach easily from their plugs. Raspberries do not store well and are at their best when freshly picked. The challenge is often to get them to the kitchen before eating them all *en route*. Picking should be done on a dry day and the fruits should be put in shallow layers in the container; deep layers will damage the berries. Berries will store in the refrigerator for a few days and will freeze very well if there are any to spare. Place the berries in shallow trays in the freezer and transfer them to plastic bags once frozen.

Blackberries and Hybrid Berries

Blackberries have provided sustenance to humans for millennia. An analysis of a bog-preserved body of a Danish woman who died 2,500 years ago revealed that blackberries had been part of her last meal.

The blackberry is a close botanical relative of the raspberry and is an established native plant widespread in the United Kingdom. Foraging for wild blackberries is a popular and often productive pastime, but is not without its drawbacks. The barbarous thorns of the blackberry can give painful scratches and snag clothing. Modern varieties of blackberry do not differ greatly from their wild cousins except that many are thornless, have erect rather than floppy stems, and are more productive.

There is widespread debate amongst fruit growers as to whether the modern varieties have the same flavour as their wild counterparts. This is hard to prove, partly because wild blackberries are not a single variety, but genetically are very diverse, and their flavour is not standard. From personal experience, cultivated blackberries provide a nutritious and flavoursome crop and are much easier to harvest than the wild types.

The flowers of blackberries are attractive and are visited frequently by pollinating insects. The foliage of the variety Oregon Thornless is attractive and the plant can be valued for its ornamental as well as its cropping attributes.

Blackberries and raspberries are capable of hybridisation – the first recorded instance was in California in the nineteenth century in a garden belonging to Judge Logan. The judge noticed a seedling that happened to be a blackberry/raspberry cross and cultivated the plant. The resultant fruit was large with a delicious flavour, sharper than a raspberry but still good for eating fresh.

There have been several other hybrid berries that have been developed. In 1979 the tayberry was introduced by the Scottish Horticultural Research Institute. This is a raspberry/blackberry hybrid, and the fruit is a little sweeter than that of loganberries but sharper than raspberries. The tayberry has proved to be a reliable choice for British growers.

Boysenberries originate from a cross involving the raspberry, the blackberry and the American dewberry. The black fruits are credited with a wild blackberry flavour, and cropping is heavy. Boysenberries are quite tolerant of dry soil.

The tummelberry comes from an unknown cross in which the tayberry was one parent. They are redder than tayberries and ripen slightly later. The fruits resemble large raspberries. Tummelberries fare well in northern areas.

Except for the blackberry variety Reuben, blackberries and hybrid berries are all floricane types, flowering and fruiting on growth made the previous season.

Selected Varieties

All the varieties listed are thornless.

Blackberry Loch Ness – a high-yielding thornless variety that is very popular with commercial growers.

Blackberry Reuben – a primocane variety that fruits on first-year canes. Pruning is relatively simple.

Apache

Apache is a mid-season blackberry variety with erect canes cropping from mid-July onwards.

Loch Ness

Like most of the modern blackberry varieties, Loch Ness has erect stems. It is early cropping, it produces large berries in abundance, and is favoured by commercial growers. Cropping extends from mid-August until the first frosts.

Oregon Thornless

Oregon Thornless is a deservedly popular variety that is both ornamental and productive. The handsome semi-evergreen foliage and attractive white flowers make this variety a great choice for growing against a sunny fence or wall. It is moderately vigorous and suitable where space is restricted. Cropping is in late August.

Reuben

The blackberry variety Reuben is remarkable as it is one of the few primocane blackberry varieties that crop on the current season's growth. The large berries can be harvested from mid-July onwards.

Waldo

Waldo is an early variety that crops in mid-July. Its growth is compact so it is a good choice for garden cultivation.

Planting and Cultivation

Blackberries and hybrid berries fare best when given a post-and-wire support system as described for raspberries. They prefer a sunny position, but blackberries can tolerate light shade. Late autumn and early winter are the best times for planting, and soil enrichment using well-rotted manure is beneficial.

Apart from the primocane variety Reuben, the previous season's growth and new growth are kept separate to facilitate harvesting and pruning. New growth can be trained up through the centre of the plant, with older fruiting growth moved to the outside. This can be done by placing the previous year's canes near the base of the plant and training the new growth between the canes up through the middle of the plant, using soft twine to keep them in place.

Once the canes have cropped, they are cut out completely. This is best done by cutting them into sections before removing them. Once the fruited canes have been removed, all side growth arising from the current season's canes should be shortened back to 5cm (2in) before tying them into the post-and-wire support. This growth should be spread out, allowing space for the new canes to grow through the centre of the plant.

Primocane varieties such as Reuben have all canes cut back to ground level, in much the same way as for autumn-fruiting raspberries.

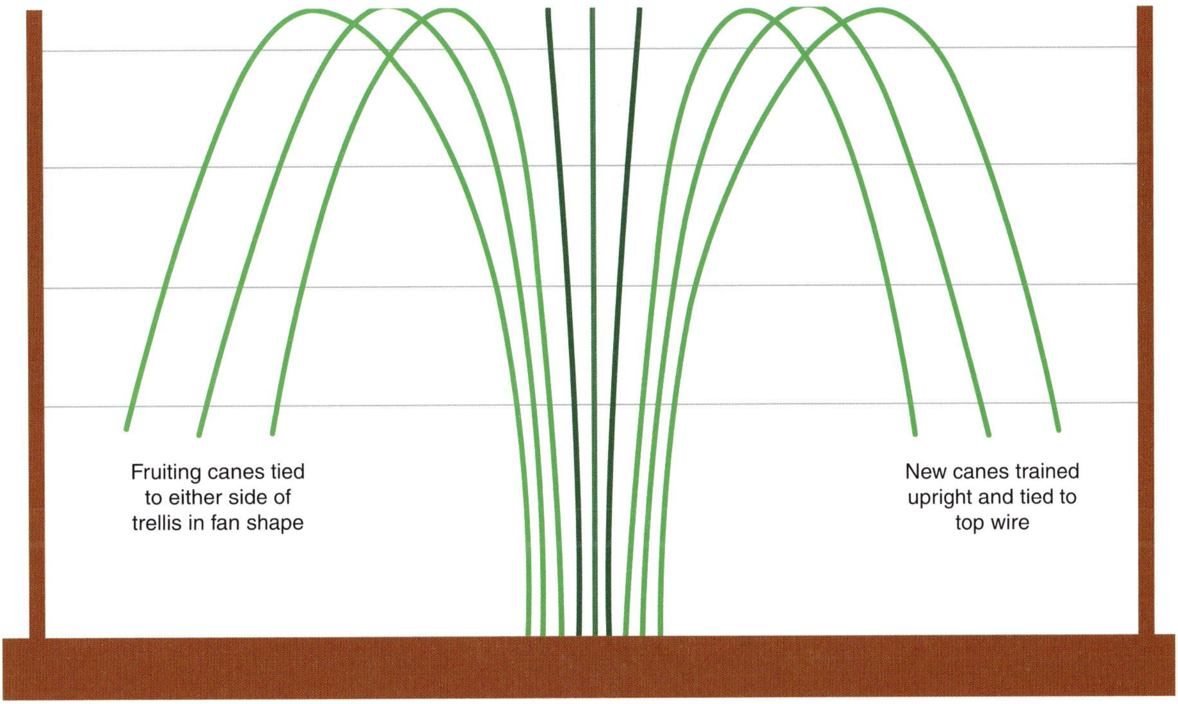

Training floricane blackberries.

Propagation

Unless large numbers of plants are required for commercial production, blackberries and hybrid berries will readily reproduce themselves by layering. If a stem from young growth is allowed to come in contact with the soil, it will readily form roots at the point of contact and continue to grow. Once the roots have established (a gentle tug on the stem will confirm this), the young plant can be detached from its parent and either potted or transferred to its new planting position. Blackberries and hybrid berries are not affected by viruses to the same extent as raspberries and so can be propagated without worry.

Hardwood cuttings taken from pieces of dormant current season's growth provide another method of propagation, especially if many plants are required. Cuttings are made about 20cm (8in) long, with a slanting cut made just above a bud and a straight cut at the base. The cuttings are inserted in a pot containing a freely draining rooting medium, with one-third of the length of the cuttings above the level of the medium. The cuttings are best prepared as soon as the stock plants become dormant, and can be placed in a cold frame to root over winter.

Diseases, Disorders and Pests

Blackberries are remarkably trouble-free in terms of pests and diseases, but share a few with raspberries, which have already been discussed under the previous section. Raspberry beetle can be a pest of hybrid and early blackberries. Phytophthora root rot may be problematic on wet soils. Blackberries may suffer from rust disease, which affects plants with congested growth in wet weather; however, it seldom causes serious problems. The large blackberry aphid, *Amphorophora rubi*, seldom causes enough damage to warrant control measures, but a natural plant-oil spray suitable for aphid control provides a simple remedy. The spotted wing drosophila (SWD) has the potential to be a serious pest of blackberries and hybrid berries, and hopefully research being carried out all over the world will provide non-chemical control methods for this insect.

Watering and Nutrition

Like most soft fruits, these plants prefer a compound feed that is biased towards potassium. A spring mulch with well-rotted manure supplemented by a potassium-rich granular fertiliser is ideal.

The soil will need watering in dry periods, but overwatering can cause a lot of problems, particularly phytophthora root rot.

Harvesting and Storage

Blackberries and hybrid berries are less fragile than raspberries as the fruit detaches with its core. The fruits are best harvested on a dry day when they are plump and fully coloured. They will store for a week in a refrigerator but are excellent for freezing or making into sauces and conserves. Blackberry wine is a favourite hedgerow wine, and blackberries can be used to flavour spirits such as brandy or whisky to make a wonderful winter drink.

CHAPTER 9

GROWING BUSH FRUITS

Bush fruits include blackcurrants, gooseberries, red- and whitecurrants, and blueberries. Blackcurrants, gooseberries and redcurrants are all members of the plant genus *Ribes* and are capable of hybridising. The jostaberry is a man-made cross between a blackcurrant and a gooseberry and shows characteristics of both parents. Whitecurrants are a variant of redcurrants (*Ribes rubrum*). Blueberries belong to the plant genus *Vaccinium*, which is a close relative of rhododendrons and heathers. Like many members of the rhododendron family (*Ericaceae*), blueberries require an acidic soil.

Blackcurrants

The blackcurrant, *Ribes nigrum*, is native in northern Europe and Asia, and has been cultivated in Britain for over 500 years. Cultivation may have occurred five centuries earlier in Russia. The fruit's importance as a valuable source of vitamin C was recognised during World War II when the fruit became invaluable due to oranges being unavailable, and blackcurrant juice was supplied free to children. Weight for weight, blackcurrants contain more than three times the amount of vitamin C than oranges. In addition, blackcurrants are rich in polyphenols, antioxidants and anthocyanins, making them both nutritious and flavoursome.

The cool, temperate UK climate is ideal for growing blackcurrants, and approximately 10,000 tonnes are grown in Britain every year. About 90 per cent of the crop is used to make cordial, with most of the remainder used to make conserves; only a small amount of fresh fruit is available to the consumer. This is a very good reason for home gardeners to grow blackcurrants to enjoy the benefits of this versatile fruit. Blackcurrants are easy to grow, and new varieties have better disease resistance and often more compact growth than their heritage counterparts. Blackcurrants are very easy to propagate without the need for specialist equipment, and a row of fruit bushes can be established for minimal cost.

Selected Varieties

Most blackcurrant varieties offered by British nurseries have been bred by the Scottish Crop Research Institute (SCRI), which has been at the forefront of blackcurrant breeding. Improved berry size and disease resistance have been the main achievements of this breeding programme, but some compact varieties have been developed, making them ideal for gardens where space is at a premium. The SCRI varieties are usually prefixed with 'Ben'. The cropping times are mainly July, so the terms 'early' or 'late cropping' are relative and there is considerable overlap between varieties. Blackcurrants are self-fertile and can provide good crops without the assistance of a pollinator.

Blackcurrant Baldwin – a traditional variety with crops of deliciously tart berries that are rich in vitamin C.

Blackcurrant Black n Red – both productive and ornamental and so can be grown in a shrub border.

Baldwin

Baldwin is one of the few heritage varieties that is still grown by many fruit nurseries. It is a mid-season variety ripening in mid-July. The berries are sharp to the taste and this variety has the reputation of being the best-flavoured blackcurrant. The thick-skinned berries are resistant to splitting, and have a high vitamin C content. For all its attributes, this variety is rather disease-prone, and its blossoms are susceptible to spring frost damage.

Ben Connan

Ben Connan is an outstanding mid-season variety with many attributes. The large berries ripening in mid-July have excellent flavour and are borne on short trusses. Frost, pest and disease resistance is good, and growth is compact.

Ben Hope

Ben Hope is a mid-season variety, ripening in the middle of July; it is especially popular with organic growers on account of its excellent pest and disease resistance. The bushes are vigorous, growing to about 2m (6.5ft) in height, and so will need more space than most other blackcurrant varieties.

Ben Lomond

This mid- to late-season variety has comparatively sweet berries on short trusses. It flowers later than most and is therefore less troubled by spring frosts. It also benefits from good mildew resistance. The compact growth makes it an excellent choice for small gardens.

Ben More

Ben More is a vigorous, late-flowering and mid- to late-fruiting variety that gives heavy crops of fruit. It is particularly useful for northern areas or locations troubled by spring frosts.

Ben Sarek

The distinctive feature of this early variety is its compact growth, making it a very good choice for a small garden. The berries are large and have a sharp flavour and are borne on short trusses. The variety has good frost and mildew resistance.

Big Ben

The variety Big Ben produces berries that are about twice the size of most others without compromising flavour. The berries ripen in mid-July and have a sweet, rich flavour. It has good resistance to leaf spot and powdery mildew.

Black n Red

Black n Red is an unusual blackcurrant variety that can be grown in an ornamental shrub border on account of its decorative foliage. The foliage starts off green in spring, and reddens as the season progresses. The fruit is deliciously sweet and ripens in mid-July. It has good resistance to leaf spot and powdery mildew.

Ebony

The outstanding feature of Ebony is the sweetness of the berries, which can be eaten fresh. The fruits are large, comparable in size to Big Ben, and can be a great ingredient in fresh fruit salads. The variety has good mildew resistance.

Foxendown

Foxendown is extremely disease-resistant and is therefore a good choice for organic growing. The flavourful berries appear on long trusses.

Titania

Titania is exceptional on account of its long cropping period, extending from early July to early August. The variety has good mildew and rust resistance.

Pollination

Blackcurrants are self-fertile but the blossoms can be damaged by spring frosts. For early-flowering varieties such as Baldwin that are grown in areas troubled by spring frosts, it is a good idea to have some horticultural fleece handy to cover the bushes on frosty nights when the bushes are in flower.

Planting and Training

Blackcurrants can be purchased as either bare-rooted or container-grown plants. Bare-rooted plants are usually considerably cheaper, but are only available when the plants are dormant in winter.

Plants should be free from virus, ideally coming from stock raised under the Fruit Propagation Certification Scheme (FPCS).

Recent research has concluded that the addition of bulky organic materials such as garden compost to the planting hole can do more harm than good; such materials should be used as a mulch after planting. The exception is in the case of very light sandy soils with poor water-holding and nutrient capacity. A balanced fertiliser such as blood, fish and bone should be applied to the surface of the soil around the base of the plant to encourage new growth.

Blackcurrants benefit from being planted deep, about 5cm (2in) deeper than they were when grown in the nursery as indicated by the 'soil mark' on bare-rooted plants, or by covering the top of the rootball with 5cm (2in) of soil on container-grown plants. This deep planting will encourage basal growth that will improve productivity.

Blackcurrants fruit on wood made in the previous growing season and therefore need a continuous supply of new growth to ensure cropping. This necessitates the removal of older wood to make way for the new.

On planting, the entire bush should be cut back hard to about 5cm (2in) above ground level. This assumes that the bush has been planted whilst dormant; if planted whilst in active growth, the operation should be carried out the following winter. Although brutal, the pruning will encourage new growth that will bear fruit on wood made in the second year after planting; however there will be no fruiting in the first year.

Pruning for the next few years will depend on the vigour of the plants. If growth is strong, pruning is simply the removal of weak, overcrowded and low-hanging shoots. If growth is weak, the bushes can be pruned harder to encourage new growth.

After about four years after planting, the aims of pruning must be to maintain the balance between old and new growth; approximately one-quarter to a third of shoots are removed just above ground level at the completion of cropping. If propagation material is required, this operation can be done as soon as the bushes become dormant.

Blackcurrants are occasionally sold as half-standard trees. These consist of the cultivated variety being grafted on to a stem of another species of *Ribes* (often *Ribes odoratum*). Half-standards make the job of picking fruit much easier but they may be more difficult to protect from frost and birds.

On grafted plants any growth arising from the rootstock (any part of the plant below the graft union) must be removed. The growth above the graft union on half-standard plants is treated in exactly the same way as bushes that are hard pruned on planting and the main shoots selectively removed.

Propagation

Blackcurrants are one of the easiest fruits to propagate by hardwood cuttings taken in late autumn. The current season's growth is selected as soon as it enters dormancy. The propagation material should be approximately pencil thickness in diameter, and a slanting cut made just above a growth bud on the top of the cutting, and a horizontal cut made at its base.

Cuttings should be about 20cm (8in) in length, and it is not necessary to make the bottom cut just below a bud as is normal practice with most cuttings. The cuttings are then inserted into a freely draining soil or growing medium where they will start to form root initials over winter. If the soil is heavy, a free-draining material such as horticultural grit should be incorporated into it so that there is sufficient oxygen to allow respiration of the tissues where rooting will occur. It is not unusual to get a 100 per cent success rate with blackcurrants. In the following spring, the cuttings can be spaced out to allow for growth and then placed in their final planting positions the following autumn.

It is unlawful to propagate varieties that are protected by plant breeders' rights without the appropriate licence.

Prepared hardwood cuttings.

Diseases and Pests

Leaf Spot

Leaf spot is a potentially serious disease caused by the fungus *Drepanopeziza ribis,* which can infect redcurrants and gooseberries as well as blackcurrants. The symptoms are small dark spots appearing on the leaves in early summer. As the disease develops the spots may merge, making large patches on the leaves. In severe infestations the foliage may drop, leaving the bushes bare by mid-July. This can have a debilitating effect on the plant and the currants may fail to develop.

Some control can be achieved by raking up and destroying fallen leaves.

The effects of this disease may be mitigated by keeping the affected plants well fed using liquid fertilisers and ensuring that they are kept watered during periods of drought.

The varieties 'Big Ben' and 'Ben Hope' show some resistance to this disease.

Rust

Although unsightly, rust rarely affects the crop. Bright orange pustules appear on the undersides of leaves, which may fall prematurely in cases of severe infestation. The disease has an alternative host of certain pine species, on which it can be more severe. The damage caused to pine trees that are important timber species was the reason that growing blackcurrants and other *Ribes* species was banned in the United States.

Powdery Mildew

Powdery mildew is a fungal disease that causes a whitish deposit on the foliage. The disease can be controlled by pruning out dense growth to allow better air circulation between the stems, and the use of mulches to reduce water stress. Products are available containing natural plant oils that can be applied as a spray to reduce powdery mildew attack.

Reversion

Reversion is a disease caused by a type of bacteria called a mycoplasma, and it is very similar to a virus in its effects. The most significant of these is a drastic reduction in cropping. It is not always easy to diagnose this disease, which is so named because the foliage of infected bushes looks as if the plant has reverted to a wild blackcurrant. The leaves of infected plants may become smaller with fewer major lobes, and the flowers may be malformed. The disease is transmitted from plant to plant by the blackcurrant gall mite. The only control is the removal and destruction of affected plants, and new blackcurrant plants must not be established in the same place where affected bushes have been removed. There is no approved chemical control for the disease or the gall mite.

Reversion of blackcurrant is hard to spot but anyway is untreatable. Destruction of the affected plants is usually the best option.

Aphids

There are three species of aphid commonly encountered on blackcurrants, but only one has a significant effect on cropping. All three species overwinter as eggs on blackcurrant bushes and hatch in spring. The currant sowthistle aphid (*Hypermyzus lactucae*) is the most significant pest and is the only one likely to warrant control measures. This aphid hatches in early spring and can rapidly develop large populations of wingless insects by asexual reproduction (parthenogenesis). The foliage becomes distorted and shows yellow mottling. In May and June the population changes from wingless to winged insects, which then migrate on to sowthistle (*Sonchus*), its summer host. In autumn, the aphids return to blackcurrants to mate and lay eggs to overwinter.

The currant blister aphid (*Cryptomyzus ribis*) causes distinctive red puckering on young foliage. The symptoms of this pest may cause alarm, but control measures are seldom warranted. In midsummer the aphid migrates to hedge woundwort (*Stachys sylvatica*), its summer host.

Hoverflies are useful predators as well as being pollinators.

Big bud is caused by the blackcurrant gall mite, which is a vector for the serious virus-like disease of reversion.

The permanent currant aphid (*Aphis schneideri*) feeds on blackcurrants for the duration of the growing season and does not have an alternative host plant. The black aphids can cause a significant reduction in the length of shoots but should not affect cropping to an extent to cause concern.

Although aphid populations can grow rapidly, large colonies of this pest bring in predators to feast on them. Ladybirds can be encouraged by companion planting, as can hoverflies. Wasps are voracious predators of aphids, as are many species of birds.

Crushing colonies of aphids between fingers and thumb is a quick way to reduce populations of the pest.

Pesticides based on natural plant oils or fatty acids provide good control without harming the environment. However, these natural pesticides have short persistence and so repeat applications may be necessary for effective control.

Blackcurrant Gall Mite

Blackcurrant gall mites feed inside the buds of blackcurrants on the embryonic leaves. Affected buds are easily identified in late winter as they become noticeably swollen. This condition is often known as 'big bud'. Affected buds may dry up and often fail to open. Mites emerge from the buds in spring and look for new buds to feed on; they may also be blown on to other blackcurrant bushes. Apart from the direct damage caused to the plant, gall mites pose a more serious threat by spreading reversion disease. There is no chemical control for gall mite, and affected buds should be picked off and destroyed as they appear in late winter. The blackcurrant variety Ben Hope has resistance to gall mites.

Blackcurrant Gall Midge

Blackcurrant gall midge is a small fly whose larvae feed on young foliage, causing it to become distorted and underdeveloped. The pest usually has three generations per year. After feeding, the larvae go into the soil to pupate. The distorted foliage may initially be mistaken for aphid damage, but a closer examination of the plants will confirm the culprit. Picking off affected foliage may do more harm than good by reducing photosynthesis. Hoeing around the base of the plants may help to reduce populations of larvae.

Birds

Birds can cause a total loss of the crop, and the only reliable solution is protective netting. Bird scarers such as kites designed to look like hawks flying high about the plants may have some effect, but birds will become accustomed to them, and the kites will lose their desired effect. If using kites as scarers, position them as late as possible to avoid birds becoming familiar with them.

Spotted Wing Drosophila (SWD)

SWD is a new pest to the UK but has the potential to be devastating. The symptoms and control of this pest have been discussed in the relevant section in Chapter 5: Growing Plums.

Watering and Feeding

Established blackcurrant bushes usually do not require irrigation, but a case could be made for when bushes have become debilitated by leaf spot during periods of dry weather. Mulching with well-rotted farmyard manure will supply plant nutrients, suppress weeds and conserve moisture. Blackcurrants are heavy feeders, and if nutrients are not supplied by manures, a balanced fertiliser should be applied to the soil surface at the specified rate. The fertiliser must contain adequate levels of nitrogen to encourage vigorous new growth that will bear flowers and fruit the following year.

Harvesting and Storage

Modern varieties of blackcurrant (such as those bred by the Scottish Crop Research Institute and prefixed with Ben) were developed for mechanical harvesting, and so all the berries would ripen at the same time. When grown in the garden, the entire truss can be picked. The berries of older varieties such as Baldwin should be picked individually as the berries at the top of the truss tend to ripen first.

Blackcurrants will last for up to a week in a fridge, but once the stalks have been removed they will need to be used quickly. They freeze very well and can be made ready for a variety of culinary uses.

Gooseberries

Although their popularity was eclipsed in the latter part of the twentieth century, gooseberries have staged a revival in Britain. This is partly due to increased interest in cookery, and the advent of improved varieties that are sweeter and more disease-resistant, with fewer and smaller thorns. Gooseberries are native to Northern Europe and Western Asia and are probably native to Britain. Why gooseberries obtained their name is not clear: it is likely to have been a corruption of a French, German or Dutch name, with nothing to do with geese.

Gooseberries have been cultivated in Britain for centuries in cottage gardens, but it was in the late eighteenth century that development of new varieties was started in earnest. In northern England, gooseberry societies were formed to satisfy an almost fanatical interest in the fruit. A few remain today in which members compete to grow the largest gooseberry by stripping their bushes of all but a few berries to enable the remaining ones to become unusually large.

Gooseberries appreciate the relative cool and damp British climate. Hot, dry conditions do not suit them well, and the UK is the third largest producer of gooseberries in the world, trailing behind Russia and Ukraine.

A close relative of the blackcurrant (*Ribes nigrum*), the gooseberry (*Ribes uva-crispa*) is a host plant for rust disease of pines, and its cultivation is controlled or prohibited in the United States.

Gooseberry varieties are usually classified as dessert (suitable for eating fresh), and culinary or cooking varieties that usually need sweetening when cooked for desserts. Some varieties are dual-purpose, and green, immature fruits are picked for cooking and the rest allowed to develop into large, sweet fruits for eating fresh weeks later.

Selected Varieties

Gooseberry Captivator – the sweet red berries of this excellent variety can be eaten fresh and make a great addition to fruit salads.

Gooseberry Invicta – a good disease-resistant culinary variety with reliable and heavy cropping.

Gooseberry Hinnomaki Red – yields sweet fruit that can be eaten fresh, and it makes a great addition to a fruit salad.

Captivator (Dessert)

Captivator is a new variety from Canada that has many attributes. The red fruits are deliciously sweet when ripe and can be eaten fresh, and make a great ingredient in a fresh fruit salad. This variety has very small thorns and has good mildew resistance.

Greenfinch (Cooking)

Greenfinch is a compact growing variety with good disease resistance. The thorns are relatively small. It produces reliable crops of green berries slightly earlier than most varieties.

Hinnonmaki Red (Dessert)

Like Captivator, this variety from Finland has small thorns and good mildew resistance, and produces small red fruits. It is recommended for organic growing on account of its disease resistance. The variety 'Hinnonmaki Yellow' is similar but with yellow rather than red fruits.

Invicta (Cooking)

Invicta is a heavy-cropping, large-fruited green gooseberry with good mildew resistance. Growth is vigorous and the thorns large and spiteful, but its reliability makes it a good choice of variety.

Leveller (Dual-Purpose)

Leveller is an old variety popular with exhibition growers. The berries can be picked green for cooking and the remainder left to ripen fully with large, sweet fruits.

Martlett (Dual-Purpose)

Like most modern varieties, Martlett has good mildew resistance. The red berries are deliciously sweet when fully ripened.

Whinham's Industry (Dessert)

Whinham's Industry is an old variety and rather prone to mildew. It is relatively shade-tolerant and can crop heavily. The bright red berries are good for eating fresh when fully ripe, and the flavour is outstanding.

Pollination

Gooseberries are self-fertile so no pollinators are required.

Planting, Pruning and Training

Like blackcurrants, gooseberries can be purchased as standard plants, with the cultivated gooseberry variety grafted on to a stem of a vigorous species of *Ribes*. The gooseberry part of the plant can be treated in the same way as a bush gooseberry in terms of pruning. Gooseberries can be trained as vertical cordons (either single or double), or fans for gracing a wall.

Gooseberries can also be used to make an attractive, informal hedge. When pruning a gooseberry hedge, it is important not to allow the growth to become too dense otherwise it will adversely affect the quality of the fruit and encourage mildew.

Pruning Bush Gooseberries

Bush gooseberries are often grown on a short stem, as this will keep framework shoots away from the soil and prevent fruits from coming into contact with it and rotting. If buying plants, try and select bushes that have a short stem before the framework shoots develop. This may be achieved by removing low-growing branches off the main stem. The length of this stem should be between 20 and 30cm (8 and 12in).

It is possible to grow gooseberries without having a short stem, however pruning cuts may need to be made to an upward-facing bud to discourage downward growth.

Four or five framework shoots are selected, and these are shortened to 15 to 20cm (6 to 8in) in length in winter. In early summer side shoots should be pruned back to five leaves, and the framework shoots left unpruned.

The following winter, the side shoots are pruned to three buds and the framework shoots pruned back by a quarter. This pruning system is repeated in subsequent years. Alternatively, a simpler pruning system can be adopted in which crossing and congested growth is removed during winter.

Pruning Cordon Gooseberries and Fans

Cordon gooseberries are an efficient way of growing the fruit if space is limited, and provide better access to the berries without having to reach into thorny bushes. For some varieties, such as Invicta, this is a big bonus!

It is not easy to buy cordon gooseberries, so these are best grown from hardwood cuttings made the previous year. As with all cordon fruits, a strong post-and-wire structure is required to support the cordons. The end posts should be braced, and strong horizontal wires at 50cm (20in) spacings should be attached to posts and strained. The upper wire should be about 1.7m (5.6ft) from the ground. The cordons should be attached to vertical canes, which are attached to the horizontal wires.

Cuttings with long leading shoots are selected and pruned back by a quarter to just above a bud. All side growths that are lower than 15cm (6in) are removed, and the remainder are pruned back to two buds. If a double cordon is required, the leading shoots should be pruned back by a half, and two resultant shoots selected to form the double cordon.

After the initial winter pruning, in the following summer all young side shoots are shortened back to five leaves and the leading shoot(s) are tied into the canes. Once the cordons have reached the uppermost supporting wire, the extension growth should be shortened to five leaves in early summer and one bud in winter.

The training and pruning of gooseberry fans follow the same principles already described for fan-trained fruit.

Propagation

Like blackcurrants, gooseberries can be propagated easily by hardwood cuttings that are prepared at the onset of dormancy in late autumn. The cutting should be taken from leafless current season's growth. If a short stem is required, the cuttings are inserted more shallowly in soil or growing medium than is usual for hardwood cuttings, with only a third of the cutting inserted into the medium. The cuttings should be left outside in winter when they will start to form root initials. Once rooting has occurred, the cuttings may be transferred to their permanent positions.

Diseases and Pests

American Gooseberry Mildew

American gooseberry mildew is the most common and harmful disease of gooseberries. Affected foliage and stems become covered in a white fungal deposit that sometimes affects the fruit. The best control for this common disease is the selection of resistant varieties such as Greenfinch and Invicta. Cutting out affected stems will help to control the disease. Natural plant oils that can be used to control aphids have some effect in controlling powdery mildews and are considered environmentally safe.

Gooseberry Sawfly

The caterpillars of gooseberry sawfly can strip the foliage of gooseberry bushes at an alarmingly fast rate, leaving just the leaf veins. The damage starts in late spring, but as there can be up to three generations per year of this pest, feeding can continue throughout the summer. The main method of control is by removing the caterpillars, which requires constant vigilance and close inspection of the bushes.

Spotted Wing Drosophila (SWD)

Although new to the UK, the threat from this potentially serious pest is increasing. The symptoms and control of SWD have been discussed in Chapter 5: Growing Plums.

Birds

Birds such as pigeons can strip the fruit from gooseberry bushes resulting in an almost total loss of the crop. Bird scarers may have a temporary effect, but the best solution is to use bird-proof netting.

Watering and Feeding

Gooseberries are appreciative of a generous mulch of organic material such as well-rotted farmyard manure or home-made compost every spring. A potassium-rich general fertiliser should be applied at this time to assist fruit production and disease resistance. Established gooseberry bushes growing in anything but the lightest of soils should not need watering except during periods of extended drought. Gooseberries growing in containers will need regular watering and liquid feeding during the growing season.

Harvesting and Storage

Gooseberries are normally picked twice: in June, every other fruit is picked for cooking, allowing the remainder to swell and sweeten to be picked from mid-July onwards. Gooseberries can be kept in a refrigerator for a couple of weeks but are excellent for freezing. It is important to pick the ripe fruits carefully as they are easily crushed.

Gooseberry sawfly defoliates gooseberry bushes and reduces their cropping potential.

Redcurrants and Whitecurrants

Redcurrants are native to Western Europe and thrive in the relatively cool and moist British climate. Although valued by physicians in the Middle Ages, the development of improved varieties of redcurrants began in France and the Low Countries in the seventeenth century.

Redcurrants are rich in vitamins C and K, and have a pleasant mix of sweetness and acidity. They are most associated with redcurrant jelly, which is used as an accompaniment for meats, particularly lamb; however, a renewed interest in cookery has seen an increase in the popularity of redcurrants as an ingredient for sauces and desserts.

Redcurrants in Britain are derived from the species *Ribes rubrum*, and whitecurrants belong to the same species, as they are an albino form of this fruit but have slightly sweeter berries. Both can make a fantastic and colourful combination for summer fruit salads. Both red- and whitecurrants need the same cultivation.

Redcurrants crop on older wood, much like gooseberries, and so their training and pruning is very similar. Like gooseberries, redcurrants can be purchased as standards or bushes, ideally on a short stem to keep the trusses of red fruits off the soil. They can also be grown as cordons and fans where space is restricted.

Selected Redcurrant Varieties

Redcurrant Jonkheer van Tet – a heavy-cropping, early-fruiting variety of redcurrant.

Redcurrant Laxton's Number One – a traditional variety that flowers late and so is less likely to be damaged by frosts.

Jonkheer van Tet

Jonkheer van Tet is an early variety that makes vigorous growth and is recommended for growing as cordons.

Junifer

Junifer is a very early cropping variety producing masses of easily picked fruit. The growth is upright, and it has good resistance against leaf spot.

Laxton's Number One

Laxton's Number One is a long-established early variety with long strings of large berries. It is a reliable cropper.

Redstart

This late variety was bred at the East Malling Research Station in Kent. It is a heavy-cropping variety that makes compact growth, so it is a good choice for small gardens.

Red Lake

Red Lake is a mid-season variety producing masses of bright red, shiny fruits.

Rovada

Rovada is the most popular variety amongst commercial growers on account of its high yields. It is a late-season cropper with good-quality fruit.

Selected Whitecurrant Varieties

Whitecurrant Blanka – a very heavy-cropping, late-fruiting variety.

Blanka

Blanka is a heavy-cropping, late-season variety with ivory-coloured fruits.

Versailles Blanche (White Versailles)

This variety is one of the first whitecurrants to crop, and produces reliable yields of pale yellow, sweet berries.

Pollination

Red- and whitecurrants are self-fertile and do not need a pollinator.

Planting and Training

Redcurrants grown as bushes are normally given 1.5m (5ft) spacings; as single cordons the spacing is 0.5m (1.6ft). Redcurrants, like gooseberries, crop on older wood, and their formative and maintenance pruning is identical to that of gooseberries, already described earlier in this chapter, though usually six framework shoots are selected for bush redcurrant and whitecurrant plants. The short stem or 'leg' is important for redcurrants to stop the fruit from coming in contact with the soil and rotting.

Propagation

Red- and whitecurrants, like most members of the genus *Ribes*, are easily propagated by hardwood cuttings made as soon as the plants become dormant in late winter. As with gooseberries, cuttings are made as long as possible to accommodate the short stem at the base of the plant. Cuttings made 30cm (12in) long are ideal, and inserted to a depth of about 10cm (4in) into soil or compost. A slanting cut should be made just above a bud. During winter, rooting will start, and by early spring, small roots should appear at the base of the cuttings. The cutting can be transferred to its permanent planting position. For redcurrants grown as bushes, about six strong shoots at least 15cm (6in) above ground should be selected to form the framework shoots the following winter. These should be shortened by one third, and all other growth removed. Subsequent pruning follows the system explained for gooseberries.

Diseases and Pests

Redcurrants are probably the least trouble of any of the soft fruits in terms of pest and disease problems. They occasionally suffer from American gooseberry mildew, whose control has been discussed in the section on gooseberries. Gooseberry sawflies can attack the foliage of redcurrants but not to the same extent as gooseberries. Aphids may also make an appearance but can be easily controlled by the use of natural plant oils or fatty acids, which have little effect on the environment. Bullfinches may attack the fruit buds in winter, and this may warrant the use of nets as a protection. The nets should be removed in spring and reinstated as the fruit ripens, as many species of bird will gorge themselves on the attractive and nutritious fruit. The spotted wing drosophila is a potentially serious pest; its control has been discussed in Chapter 5: Growing Plums.

Watering and Feeding

A generous mulch applied round the base of the bushes in spring will help to retain soil moisture, suppress weeds and supply soil nutrients. Well-rotted farmyard manure or garden compost are ideal. A potassium-rich general fertiliser will help to promote fruit production.

Established redcurrant bushes, especially those that have been mulched, will seldom need watering except during periods of drought.

Harvesting and Storage

Redcurrants are harvested when the berries have become plump and juicy by removing the whole strig. This will avoid damaging the delicate berries and reducing their storage life. The berries will keep for a week in a refrigerator, and freeze very well.

Jostaberries and Worcesterberries

These two fruits have features in common with both blackcurrants and gooseberries: the jostaberry, *Ribes* × *culverwellii*, is a man-made hybrid between a gooseberry and a blackcurrant, whereas the worcesterberry, *Ribes divaricatum*, is a natural North American species. Both fruits are very vigorous, but despite the boasts made in nursery catalogues, they can be rather disappointing in terms of productivity. They may make interesting curiosities and provide interesting fruits, but neither is worthy of mass cultivation. The vigour and barbarous thorns of the worcesterberry can make it a useful thorny hedge.

Blueberries

Wild blueberries were eaten by the first nation people of North America, who prized these nutritious fruits for both eating fresh and drying for winter. In the early twentieth century, efforts were made to develop varieties with larger fruits than the wild types. The breeding programmes were successful, and blueberries became a runaway success as a commercial crop. Although the USA is by far the main producer of blueberries, the crop is now grown throughout the world, including Western Europe. Blueberries have been credited with containing many useful nutrients, including antioxidants, as well as being absolutely delicious. Blueberries are an excellent choice for garden cultivation, having attractive flowers and colourful autumnal foliage.

Blueberries originate from several species in the plant genus *Vaccinium*, making them close relatives of rhododendrons. Like rhododendrons, blueberries require an acid soil to thrive. Soil acidity is measured on the pH scale, with any value below seven being acidic and anything above being alkaline. The pH scale is a logarithmic one – in other words, one point on the scale represents a ten-fold increase or decrease in acidity.

Jostaberry – a vigorous plant, but cropping can be moderate.

Blueberries can provide rich autumn colour in addition to tasty fruit.

Plants such as blueberries that have adapted to growing in acidic soils are used to being able to access certain soil nutrients such as iron very easily, but find them harder to absorb when growing in neutral or alkaline soils. The optimal pH for blueberries is 5.5, and a simple soil pH testing kit can be bought at most garden centres. These work by adding a soil sample to an indicator solution that changes colour according to the soil pH. The resultant colour of the indicator solution is compared to a colour chart to determine the soil pH. A more accurate result can be obtained with a glass electrode pH meter.

Alkaline soils with a pH of greater than seven are unsuited to growing blueberries, and plants should be grown in containers using a low pH (ericaceous) compost. Soil-less composts tend to lose their effectiveness after a couple of years, so an ericaceous John Innes-type compost containing loam is a much better bet.

Selected Varieties

Blueberry Chandler – a variety with very large berries that provides ornament with its vivid autumn colour and spring flowers.

Blueberry Pink Lemonade gives an attractive colour variant. It is a mid- to late-season variety with rich, pink, delicious berries. The spring flowers add colour to the garden.

Blueberry Northland – an excellent early mid-season variety with reliable crops of small, sweet berries. It is a good choice for growing in colder areas.

Blueberry Patriot – an early blueberry variety that is great for eating fresh and is suitable for growing in most parts of the UK. The autumn colour of the foliage is impressive.

Blueberry Sunshine Blue – a dwarf blueberry usually ripening in mid-July. The plant is semi-evergreen, and its compact habit makes it excellent for growing in pots.

Most cultivated blueberries are cultivars of *Vaccinium corymbosum*, the northern high bush type that forms a deciduous shrub about 1.5m (5ft) in height. More compact varieties have been bred by hybridising *Vaccinium corymbosum* with the low bush *Vaccinium angustifolia*.

In northern areas, the growing season may not be long enough for late varieties to ripen. Early fruiting varieties such as Northland are ideal in these locations.

Bluecrop

Bluecrop is a favourite with commercial growers and produces heavy crops of fruits in late August. It is a vigorous grower and has good disease resistance. The berries have good storage properties.

Chandler

Chandler is a vigorous and deservedly popular variety that is both ornamental and productive, with attractive white flowers in spring and vibrant autumn colour. The berries are large and well flavoured.

Darrow

Darrow is a mid- to late-cropping variety that is remarkable for the size of the berries; these have a slightly tart flavour.

Northland

Northland is one of the hardiest varieties of blueberry, and ripening in July, it is ideal for northern parts of the UK. The berries are small and sweet.

Patriot

Ripening in early July, Patriot is a good variety for all areas of the UK, including the north. The large berries are slightly flat. It is a good variety for eating fresh.

Pink Lemonade

Pink Lemonade is a mid- to late-ripening variety with sweet pink berries that provide an attractive colour variant.

Spartan

Spartan is a good early-cropping variety with sweet but tangy berries.

Sunshine Blue

Sunshine Blue is a compact variety that is great for restricted spaces or growing in containers. The semi-evergreen foliage has a bluish tinge, and the pale pink flowers in spring add to the ornamental features of this variety. Cropping is from mid-July onwards. This is the only truly self-fertile blueberry, and will crop well without a pollinator.

Pollination

Most blueberry varieties are partially self-fertile and will produce a crop without a pollinator; however, cropping is improved considerably by the presence of a pollinating variety. Of the named varieties, only Sunshine Blue can be considered self-fertile.

Planting and Training

Blueberries need an acid soil or compost with a pH of about 5.5 or slightly lower to flourish. For soils with a pH of slightly more than 5.5, acidification is beneficial. Sulphur chips can be incorporated into the soil before planting, and acidifying organic materials such as composted pine needles or composted sawdust will also help to lower the pH of the soil. Some commonly used organic materials such as rotted farmyard manure and mushroom compost are unsuitable as these tend to be alkaline.

Blueberries like a moist soil that is not prone to waterlogging, and heavy clay soils should be improved using a low pH medium such as ericaceous compost prior to planting. After planting, an acidic mulch of composted pine bark or composted woodchip will help to retain moisture, suppress weeds and maintain soil acidity.

If your soil has a pH of 6.5 or greater, it is advisable to plant blueberries in a container using an acidic (ericaceous) growing medium. Soil-less composts are cheaper but do not last as well as those containing soil, such as the John Innes types. Large pots need less maintenance than small ones as they are less inclined to dry out during hot summer days.

For the first two years, the only pruning that is required is the removal of weak, congested and rubbing growths. Following this, one-quarter of the stems should be taken out to near ground level or a lower replacement shoot. This should maintain the correct balance between older and young wood.

Propagation

Blueberries can be easily propagated by either softwood or semi-ripe cuttings in summer. As with all propagation, it is essential to ensure that the plant you wish to propagate is not of a variety protected by Plant Breeders' Rights. The label on the original plant will often state whether it is a protected variety; failing that, a simple internet search can confirm whether it is or not.

Softwood stem cuttings are prepared from young growth in spring. If the mother plant has been properly pruned, it will be encouraged to make this growth. Softwood cuttings lose water very quickly and it is a good idea to have everything ready so they can be inserted into the rooting medium as soon as possible after preparation.

The mother plant should be well watered, ideally the night before the cuttings are taken. A pot or seed tray is filled close to its top with a lightly consolidated rooting mixture consisting of one part perlite to one part seed compost by volume. It is a good idea to damp down the perlite prior to use as the dry material can emit an irritating dust.

Cuttings of non-flowering shoots about 10cm (4in) long are taken from the parent plant, cutting just above a leaf joint. This is best done using a sharp knife or a clean pair of secateurs. The base of the cutting is trimmed just below a leaf joint (node) using a sharp knife. The resultant cutting should be between 5 and 10cm (2 and 4in) in length. The lower leaves from the stem should be carefully removed using the knife so that when the cutting is inserted, no leaves are buried; otherwise they will rot, and this will spread to the cutting as a whole. The soft tip of the cuttings should also be removed. The rest of the foliage must be retained so that the cutting is able to photosynthesise, so that it can grow roots.

The cutting is inserted into the rooting mixture using a dibber or thin cane so that the remaining leaves are not touching the medium and the cutting can remain vertical. Other cuttings are inserted so that they do not touch each other. If available, place the seed tray or pot into a propagator after the cuttings have been inserted. An electric propagator supplying a small amount of bottom heat is ideal but an unheated propagator will work almost as well. If no propagator is available, a clear polythene bag placed over the pot is a reasonable compromise. The cuttings should be moved to a light location such as a windowsill, but must not be subjected to strong, direct sunlight. Horticultural fleece can be used to shield the cuttings from strong sunlight.

The cuttings should be inspected daily, and any showing signs of rotting or dying should be removed immediately. Plastic bags should be removed and put back twice a week to allow for ventilation to discourage the development of fungi. Rooting should take place between two and four weeks. Rooting can be detected by the slight resistance that can be felt if a cutting is pulled gently upwards.

Soon after rooting has occurred, the cuttings should be potted into 9cm (3.5in) pots in an ericaceous potting compost. The cuttings should be slowly acclimatised to lower temperatures and higher light levels before positioning outside. The young plants should be moved to a protected position for their first winter before moving to their permanent position in spring.

Semi-ripe cuttings are prepared in a similar manner from new non-flowering growth, but should be made later in the season when the base of the shoot has started to stiffen but the tip remains soft. They are usually made a little longer, about 10 to 15cm (4 to 6in) in length.

Diseases, Disorders and Pests

Blueberries are comparatively disease- and pest-free, which is part of their appeal for gardeners.

Powdery Mildew

This fungal disease is easily identified by white fungal deposits on the leaves. It is encouraged by dense growth with poor air circulation around the stems. Correct pruning to reduce the density of the stems and a mulch applied in spring to conserve soil moisture will help to reduce outbreaks of this disease.

Iron Deficiency

Iron is an important plant nutrient, and its availability is reduced in soils with a high pH. Plants such as blueberries that require acid soils can extract iron easily on account of its solubility at low pH levels. When the pH becomes either neutral or alkaline iron becomes less readily available, and blueberries are unable to absorb the iron that they need. The old-fashioned remedy of putting rusty nails round the base of the plant will not work as the issue is the solubility of the iron, rather than the amount of it in the soil.

The remedy is to use a chelated or sequestered iron fertiliser. Chelated iron remains soluble at relatively high pH values, and is usually incorporated into specialist feeds for acid-loving plants.

Aphids

Aphid populations build up quickly on host plants and develop resistance to synthetic chemical pesticides. If possible, allow natural predation by insects such as hoverfly larvae, ladybirds and wasps. Whereas each aphid species generally feeds on a narrow range of plants, aphid predators will feed on a wide range of different aphids. *A Gardener's Guide to Sustainable Gardening* by Doug Stewart (The Crowood Press, 2023) provides some excellent advice on how to encourage garden predators.

Insecticides based on natural plant oils will give some control of aphids, but these products have low persistence and may need frequent application to give effective control. Some of these plant-based insecticides will contain a growth stimulant to mitigate the effects of the pest.

Spotted Wing Drosophila

The control of this potentially serious pest has been discussed in Chapter 5: Growing Plums.

Birds

Birds appreciate nutritious and tasty blueberries and will show no restraint if allowed access to the ripe fruit. Netting the bushes is essential to avoid serious losses.

Watering and Feeding

Blueberries should be kept moist throughout the growing season and any watering should be done with harvested rainwater rather than tap water, unless this is soft and does not contain lime. The absence of limescale on the kettle element and a simple pH test will confirm this.

For plants growing in soil, an application of ammonium sulphate at the rate of 15g per square metre will encourage healthy growth and help to acidify the soil. For plants growing in containers, a liquid ericaceous feed containing chelated iron and other minerals should be applied in accordance with the manufacturer's guidance throughout the growing season.

Harvesting and Storage

Blueberries can be picked when their colour changes from green to dusky blue. They can be kept for up to two weeks in a refrigerator, and are excellent for freezing.

CHAPTER 10

GROWING VINES

Humans have cultivated and foraged vine fruits for millennia. Vineyards existed over six thousand years ago in south-east Europe and Asia, and grape cultivation spread across Europe assisted by civilisations such as the Greeks and Romans. There are numerous biblical references to grapes, and both the Greeks and Romans had gods of wine, such was the importance of the drink.

Vines are all members of the plant genus *Vitis*, which has nearly eighty species distributed throughout Europe, Asia and North America. Some species produce edible fruit and others are prized for ornamental foliage that often assumes a rich colouration in autumn. Vines are easily incorporated into the ornamental garden as they can be used to great effect to cover walls and scramble through pergolas and trellises.

The most popular vine fruit is the grape *Vitis vinifera*, which is used to make wine. Other species of *Vitis* are also cultivated for wine production, but most viticulturists agree that the best wines are made from the fruits of *Vitis vinifera*. Most grape production is devoted to winemaking, with juice production, and fresh and dried fruits being a much smaller proportion of the total harvest.

The Romans cultivated vines for winemaking in England as far north as Yorkshire, and this county has a renewed interest in grape production due to milder winters and warmer summers. In Scandinavia, commercial vineyards are springing up in Norway, Sweden, Finland and Denmark.

Settlers from Europe introduced *Vitis vinifera* to North America in order to grow grapes for winemaking, but the plant suffered from attacks by Phylloxera, a native insect related to aphids that mainly attacks the root system of vines. The importation of North American vines inadvertently introduced the pest to Europe, and it soon became widespread, causing devastation to the local wine industry.

The natural resistance of the North American *Vitis* species provided a solution, as vines grafted on to resistant rootstocks derived from them provided an effective method of controlling Phylloxera.

Vines grown for commercial grape production are invariably grafted on to a Phylloxera-resistant root-stock.

Vines can make an attractive as well as productive covering for fences.

It is much cheaper to produce vines from hardwood cuttings, but as Phylloxera is a pest that is very difficult to control, it is good policy to spend a little more and buy grafted plants.

The introduction of new, hardier varieties combined with climate change has enabled gardeners to grow grapes outside the south of England. There are still many popular varieties of grape that are best cultivated in a greenhouse and which are featured in nursery catalogues, but there are also several new varieties that can be grown outdoors in southern England. It is generally recommended that grapes grown for eating fresh are grown under glass, and those for winemaking can be grown outdoors in warmer locations, however some newer varieties are suitable for eating fresh when grown outdoors on a sunny wall.

Selected Varieties

Grapevine Phoenix – this hybrid vine is very popular with amateur growers in the UK and is easy to grow against a sunny wall.

Grapevine Regent – a popular outdoor grape. The blue-black grapes will turn pure black in a good summer and are usually sweet enough to eat fresh. The autumn colour is a bonus.

Grapevine Strawberry – a reliable and productive cropper.

Grapevine Brandt – this outdoor grape has spectacular autumn colour and is often just grown as an ornamental plant. It also produces large bunches of sweet, blue-black grapes.

The following varieties have been selected for growing outdoors in a warm, sunny location. The favourable microclimate of a south- or west-facing wall provides an ideal location. Grapes are self-fertile and do not need a pollinating variety.

Bacchus

The variety Bacchus has found favour with many commercial vineyards. It produces a good-quality white wine, but may be eaten fresh in a good year.

Boskoop Glory

The black grape Boskoop Glory is a good dual-purpose variety for both eating fresh and winemaking. The flavour is good, and it has notable disease resistance.

Brandt

Brandt is often grown as a purely ornamental climbing plant. The small grapes are full of pips so it is not good for eating fresh, but it can be made into juice. The autumn colour is excellent.

New York Muscat

New York Muscat is a good dessert variety and is particularly suitable for growing on a warm wall. The black grapes have a distinct blackcurrant flavour, and the variety has good disease resistance.

Phoenix

Phoenix is a very good variety for the amateur grower. The grapes are large, and they ripen early and so are not as dependent on the vagaries of the British weather as other varieties that ripen later in autumn when sunshine and warmth are becoming increasingly scarce. Disease resistance is good, and it is one of the best dessert varieties for growing in warmer parts of England and Wales.

Regent

Regent is a black grape suitable for eating fresh, but it can be used for wine. Disease resistance is good, and the autumn foliage makes an impressive display.

Strawberry

Strawberry is an easily grown and productive variety also known as 'Fragola'. The sweet fruits have a hint of strawberry, and cropping is reliable.

Suffolk Red

Despite its name, Suffolk Red is a variety bred in the USA. Its red grapes are seedless and have a pleasant, sweet flavour. It is a good dessert variety but can be used for winemaking. The autumn colouration of the foliage is very attractive.

Planting

Vines require a warm microclimate to succeed, and this is particularly true for dessert grapes. The ornamental properties of vines make them ideal subjects for growing on sunny walls or scrambling over arbours or pergolas. A south- or west-facing wall will have the right microclimate to encourage ripening of the grapes with the required sugar content.

If planting against a wall or fence, the vine should be planted about 60cm (24in) from the base of the wall or fence and angled towards it. Strong wires should be attached to the wall or fence using eyelets and spaced at 30cm (12in) intervals. This should provide adequate support.

If a small vineyard is required rather than one or two vines, a post-and-wire framework will be needed. This will not have the same visual appeal of a wall-trained vine or one scrambling over trellis, but it can be a very productive arrangement.

A novel way of growing grapes is to grow the plant as a standard, where the main framework consists of a vertical stem approximately 1.5m (5ft) in length, at the top of which four or five short stems emerge. These short stems will bear the new growth that will carry the fruit. A standard grape can make a very attractive specimen for growing in a large pot. It is possible to buy standard grapes from nurseries, but they are not cheap.

Vines grown in the open using a post-and-wire support system are usually planted about 1.5m (5ft) apart. Organic matter such as rotted manure should not be incorporated into the planting hole as this may lead to waterlogging of the roots. Organic matter may be used as a mulch to retain soil moisture and discourage powdery mildew.

Pruning and Training

Left to its own devices, a grape vine rapidly develops into a tangled mess of shoots producing small, sour grapes of very little value. Grapes fruit only on new growth and so any growth left when growth commences in spring will not bear fruit. In order to be productive, grapes need savage pruning so that plenty of space is made available for new fruit-bearing wood.

There are two main pruning systems for grapes: the Guyot and the rod-and-spur system. Both involve the hard pruning of the vine to a minimal structure, and summer pruning to allow light to reach the fruits and minimise the incidence of disease.

The Guyot system was developed in France and is the recommended system for grapes grown in the open in Britain. The main framework consists of a central stem from which one or two horizontal branches of the previous season's growth emerge. A double Guyot vine has two horizontal branches arising from the main stem, and a single Guyot has one.

New growth coming from the previous season's growth will bear the fruit. After harvesting, the horizontal arms are removed, and these are replaced by shoots that have grown during the growing season. This is the main system used by commercial growers in Britain as there is less chance of framework wood being damaged by cold weather than if using the rod-and-spur system.

For both the Guyot and the rod-and-spur pruning systems, the main framework pruning is best carried out in late November to early December. This will prevent the vines from bleeding sap, which will weaken the plants.

To train a vine using the Guyot system, the vine is trained up a cane during the growing season. Any shoots growing out of the main stem are shortened back to a single leaf. In late November to early December the vine is pruned back hard, leaving two or three buds about 40cm (16in) above ground level or the graft union. Three buds will provide the two horizontal stems and an extension shoot for a double Guyot, and two buds will provide a single horizontal stem and an extension shoot for a single Guyot. The two or three resultant shoots from the retained buds are trained up the cane, and side growths restricted to a single leaf.

The following winter, two of the shoots are selected to make the horizontal branches for a double Guyot and a single one for a single Guyot. The remaining stem is cut back to either two (single Guyot) or three buds (double Guyot).

The shoots selected to be the horizontal arms will need to be tied into the support wires using soft ties, and shortened to 60 to 90cm (24 to 36in).

During the growing season, the two or three shoots arising from the shoot that was cut back to two or three buds is trained up the cane to repeat the same process as the previous year. Vertical growth coming from the horizontal arms will be the fruit-bearing growth. This is trained vertically.

After fruiting, the horizontal arms are cut out completely, and the growth that was trained up the cane is used to make new arms and future extension growth.

When used for outdoor grapes, the rod-and-spur system (occasionally called the cordon system) is used for vines grown against walls and fences. The vine is pruned to create a low-branching palmate arrangement of permanent shoots, from which the fruiting wood emerges. These shoots are trained to fill available wall spaces and create a pleasing aesthetic. New growth from this framework will bear the fruit. In winter these shoots are cut back to a single bud to provide the fruiting wood for the next season.

Grapes should not be allowed to develop for the first three years after planting to promote the establishment of the vine.

A healthy vine growing in good conditions will make strong growth throughout the summer. In addition to winter pruning, when fruiting wood is removed, summer pruning is necessary to allow light to reach the fruit and increase its sugar content and minimise disease infection. In early summer the clusters of flowers will become visible. The fruiting stem should be shortened to two leaves beyond the flowers. Side growths, and growths made after pruning, should be shortened to one leaf.

The removal of tendrils from vines is a moot point. The reason for doing this is that this will divert energy into fruit production and make the removal of vine growth in winter easier, but tendril removal is a time-consuming task at a busy time of year.

Unless it is pruned hard, a grapevine can become an unsightly mess.

Fruit Thinning

Grapes grown for eating fresh will need thinning, and this will improve the size and sweetness of the berries. This is not necessary for wine grapes. The grapes are thinned out just after fruit set using a specialist fine-bladed tool available from garden centres or mail-order suppliers. The bunches should be thinned to maintain the conical shape of the fruit cluster. A second thinning may be necessary as the fruits increase in size.

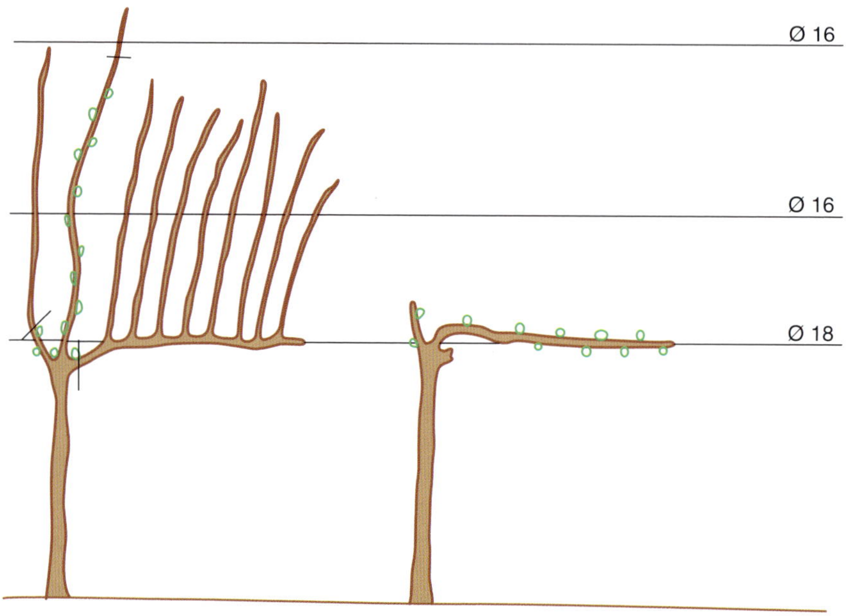

Single Guyot pruning showing the plant before and after pruning in November

Single Guyot training system.

The rod-and-spur pruning system is best used for grapes grown under glass or against walls.

Propagation

Vines are propagated by two common methods: grafting and hardwood cuttings. Grape varieties can be grafted on to a phylloxera-resistant rootstock to provide an effective control against this pest. Vines can be grafted using the whip-and-tongue or wedge graft techniques described for apples, but sourcing suitable rootstocks is not easy. Grapes root very easily from hardwood cuttings prepared in the autumn as soon as the leaves fall. Cuttings about 20cm (8in) in length are prepared with a sloping cut just above a growth bud at the top and a straight cut below a growth bud at the base. The cuttings are inserted vertically in a pot containing a rooting medium that is well aerated. A mixture of 50 per cent perlite and 50 per cent soil-less potting compost is ideal. The hardwood cuttings are left in a cold frame or cool greenhouse over winter, and should start to root in spring. After rooting, the cuttings can be potted up and grown on.

Vines are often grafted on to a rootstock to protect against phylloxera infection. The red wax protects the graft from infection.

Diseases, Disorders and Pests

Grapes grown outdoors are less troublesome than grapes grown under glass. Most pests and diseases of outdoor grapes can be controlled satisfactorily by good pruning and nutrition.

Diseases

Botrytis

Botrytis cinerea, or grey mould, is a very common fungal disease of both edible and ornamental plants, causing serious damage especially in humid conditions. For some wine growers, Botrytis is a blessing as an infection of the grapes reduces their size and increases their sugar content. The resultant wine is made sweeter and often stronger than that made with uninfected grapes. Grapes affected by Botrytis, or the 'noble rot', make dessert wines noted for their sweetness and strength. There is even a popular dessert wine variety called Botrytis.

For grapes that are eaten fresh or to be made into drier table wines, Botrytis needs to be controlled. Unfortunately there is no effective fungicide available to amateur gardeners for the control of Botrytis, so cultural methods must be used. Reducing the density of growth by careful winter as well as summer pruning will help to reduce the humidity around the plant. Reducing the use of nitrogenous fertilisers may also help to reduce infection.

Downy Mildew

Downy mildew is caused by a fungus-like organism and can be serious. Yellowish patches appear on the upper surfaces of the foliage. These patches are often limited by the veins in the leaf, and there are corresponding white patches on the undersides. This disease originated in North America and has spread globally. It is worse in wet summers. There are no chemicals available to amateur gardeners for the control of downy mildew, and so cultural control measures must be used. These include the removal and destruction of affected foliage, and pruning to reduce the density of growth.

Powdery Mildew

Powdery mildew of vines is a more common fungal disease than downy mildew in the UK and is easier to control than downy mildew. The white powdery deposits that appear mainly on the foliage are easily identifiable. The disease can be partly controlled by the use of natural plant-oil-based mildewcides (that are also used for insect control), the reduction of excessive congested growth, and mulching in spring to conserve soil moisture.

Disorders

Grapes need a warm environment that is rarely troubled by late spring frosts and which enjoys warm autumns to ripen the fruit. Late spring frosts can damage foliage and fruit buds, reducing yield. Avoiding frost pockets as planting sites and the use of horticultural fleece on nights when a late spring frost is forecast can minimise the damage. Vines can be harmed by waterlogging especially if planted in heavy clay soils. If the soil is heavy, amelioration with horticultural grit can help to reduce damage caused by waterlogging.

Vines are also prone to a variety of nutrient deficiencies, particularly manganese. Manganese deficiency is often characterised by an interveinal yellowing (chlorosis) on younger leaves. It is often associated with alkaline (high pH) soils. The best treatment for manganese deficiency is applying a liquid fertiliser containing manganese during the growing season.

Pests

Two-Spot Drosophila

This potentially serious pest from Asia arrived in Britain on imported fruit. It is now widespread in Britain. The thin skins of grapes make them very susceptible to this pest. The main method of control is the use of very fine (0.9mm) mesh to prevent the adults from reaching the fruits, and baited traps to monitor populations.

Wasps

Although wasps are useful garden predators, in late summer the adult's need for sugary sustenance makes them a nuisance when they seek fruit such as grapes. If the problem gets out of hand, a wasp trap may prove useful.

Phylloxera

Phylloxera is a small sap-sucking pest that feeds mainly on the roots of vines. It originates from North America, and it came to Europe via imported vines and rapidly became a serious pest. Many vines native to North America show a high level of resistance to this pest, and these provide the rootstocks to protect the root system of vines from attack by phylloxera. There is no chemical control for phylloxera, so the only effective method of control is to buy grafted plants.

Irrigation and Feeding

Most vines, including the grape, are tolerant of drought once established. They are considerably less tolerant of waterlogging. For the first growing season after planting, the soil should be kept moist by periodic and thorough watering. After this period there should be little need to water unless there is a period of extended drought. Adding moisture-retentive materials such as garden compost or rotted manure can cause waterlogging and must not be incorporated into the planting hole.

Grapes make vigorous growth and benefit from generous but not excessive feeding. At the commencement of growth in spring, a potassium-rich compound fertiliser should be applied round the base of each vine, supplemented by a nitrogen-rich feed when the plants are making strong growth. The fertilisers used should contain trace elements as well as the major nutrients to prevent deficiencies such as of manganese and magnesium.

Harvesting and Storage

Grapes are harvested when they have reached their required level of sweetness. For many varieties this means hanging on as late as possible, but harvesting before unfavourable weather ruins the berries. Grapes should be harvested in bunches – picking the berries individually is time-consuming, and will lead to rapid deterioration of the fruit by creating a point of entry for infection where the berry has been separated from the bunch.

Grapes can store for up to two weeks in a refrigerator. In the early twentieth century the storage life of harvested grapes was extended by allowing the stalk of a bunch of grapes to soak in water sweetened with charcoal in a horizontal bottle with an upward-turning spout. The grape storage bottle was developed by William Wood, the head gardener at Copped Hall in Essex. Unfortunately, the only grape storage bottles that remain are antique curios, but perhaps some enterprising person could develop a modern-day equivalent.

INDEX

First published in 2025 by
The Crowood Press Ltd
Ramsbury, Marlborough
Wiltshire SN8 2HR

enquiries@crowood.com
www.crowood.com

British Library Cataloguing-in-Publication Data
A catalogue record for this book is available from the British Library.

For product safety-related questions contact productsafety@crowood.com.

ISBN 978 0 7198 4539 0

Typeset by Envisage IT

Cover design by Sergey Tsvetkov

Printed and bound in India by Thomson Press

Dedication

To my five beloved grandchildren, James, Benjamin, Oliver, Zoe and Elsie.

Acknowledgements

I wish to thank Matthew Thomas, the Sales Director of Frank P. Matthews, for allowing me to take pictures of the nursery and supplying me with images of fruit varieties. I am also indebted to Stuart McIntyre of James McIntyre Nurseries for images of soft fruit varieties. Similarly, I am grateful to my two RHS colleagues, Ray Broughton and Chris Allen, for their incessant nagging to get me to complete this book. Lastly, I would like to thank Kate Scott at The Crowood Press for her support and patience that I have no doubt stretched to the limit.

Image credit

p.111: 50m. above on Unsplash.